THE TEACH
OF INITIAL LITERACY

- H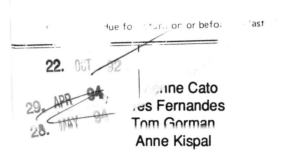DTEACHERS DO IT?

anne Cato
es Fernandes
Tom Gorman
Anne Kispal

with an appendix on children's writing at age 7
by Janet White

Published in 1992
by the National Foundation for Educational Research,
The Mere, Upton Park, Slough, Berkshire SL1 2DQ
Registered Charity No. 313392
ISBN 0 7005 1309 4

CONTENTS

Acknowledgements

I should like to thank my colleagues Anne Kispal, who was project leader from April 1990 to July 1991, and Vivienne Cato, who was leader thereafter to the end of the project in December 1991. Our thanks are due also to the project statistician, Cres Fernandes, and to Janet White, our colleague in the Centre for Research in Language and Communication, who contributed the analysis of children's writing.

We thank also Barbara Bloomfield and her colleagues in the Field Research Services Unit at the NFER for carrying out the administration of the Survey of the Teaching of Initial Literacy with their customary efficiency.

We are grateful to Ann Symmonds, together with Rajinder Jasdhoal, for wordprocessing this report and for managing our department office with such pleasant efficiency. In addition, we would like to thank Mary Hargreaves for preparing the layout, Tim Wright for designing the cover, and Enver Carim for overseeing publication of the report.

Other thanks are due to colleagues who read drafts of this report at various stages, particularly Greg Brooks, Marian Sainsbury, and Derek Foxman. We owe a particular dept of gratitude to our colleague Peter Dickson for his advice and assistance in restructuring sections of the report.

The NFER is grateful to Mr. Paul Bennians, the Director of Education in Croydon, for commissioning the Survey of the Teaching of Initial Literacy in the authority to run concurrently with the national survey. We are grateful also to Mr. Brian Howes, the Chief Inspector of Schools, and to Dr. Rosanne Simpson for cooperating closely with the research team at each stage of the enquiry in Croydon. It was a pleasure to work with officers of an authority committed to using research in the service of teaching.

Finally we would like to thank the teachers and headteachers who were willing to participate in the survey and took the time to complete our questionnaires. Special thanks are due to the teachers and pupils of the case study schools who gave much valuable time to us and, in all cases, treated us with the utmost hospitality.

Tom Gorman
Project Director

1. INTRODUCTION

1.1 The Assessment of Initial Literacy

The background of the survey of the teaching of initial literacy is to be found in research carried out between 1986 and 1989 in the Centre for Research in Language and Communication at the NFER. This research was directed towards developing a set of assessment materials that could be used to chart the progress of children aged 7-13 in the acquisition of literacy. The survey component of this earlier research, involving a nationally representative sample of pupils in Year 3, was undertaken in spring 1989. The analyses of the results showed that there was a very wide range of literacy competence among the children involved. For example, a number of children - between five and ten per cent - appeared to be unable to write independently, while a similar proportion were producing writing that compared well with the average performance of 11-year-olds. In a number of other anglophone countries, such as New Zealand, such a marked range of performance might be regarded as a cause for concern and certainly a matter for urgent investigation.

The year in which the survey took place, 1991, was the first year in which teachers of pupils in Year 2 were obliged to implement the assessment procedures associated with the National Curriculum. On the basis of the results of the trials, information is now available about the performance of pupils in Year 2 in relation to the criteria established for the attainment of levels 1 and 2 in Reading (En2) and Writing (En3). In general terms, the evidence indicates that at the end of Year 2 approximately three out of four pupils have attained at least level 2 in the Reading or Writing Standard Assessment Tasks. Those pupils who have not attained level 2 at the end of Year 2 have generally been reported to be illiterate. This is not usually the case.

The Statements of Attainment (SoAs) that characterise level 1 for Reading (En2) in the National Curriculum statutory guidelines relate to preliterate behaviour. The attainment of level 1 in reading involves no more complex attainment than the recognition of 'individual' letters or words. Attainment of level 2, on the other hand, involves reading a variety of different materials 'with independence, fluency, accuracy and understanding'. Between these two levels there are a number of 'stages' of literacy acquisition that could be designated, most significantly the movement from reading isolated words to reading continuous texts; and the transition from sub-vocalised 'word-by-word' reading to sustained 'silent' reading.

A similar knowledge divide is apparent between level 1 and level 2 in Writing (En3). Level 1 again involves 'communication' by means of isolated letters, words or phrases. Level 2 requires the independent production of written texts - a sequence of sentences, whose relationships are indicated by the appropriate punctuation.

Teachers rightly regard as literate those children who are able to read with understanding short texts on topics with which they are familiar, and to write such texts so as to be understood by others. By this definition, nine out of ten children in the survey schools could be said to have been literate at the time of the survey; but there is a wide gap between rudimentary literacy and the ability to read a range of texts aloud, accurately and fluently - an accomplishment that many adult readers do not confidently attain. The evidence in this report goes some way towards indicating how teachers assist their pupils to make the transition between these levels.

1.2 The Survey of Initial Literacy

The Survey of the Teaching of Initial Literacy took place between April 1990 and December 1991. It had two main components: a questionnaire study of a national sample of maintained schools, and case studies in a subsample of the participating schools.

The main purpose of the survey was to investigate the range of methods and approaches used by teachers in Year 2 in teaching reading and writing, and the assumptions underlying these approaches. The survey was not, therefore, specifically designed to provide evidence about 'how well six and seven year-olds read or write'. The central issue was rather: 'How are they taught to read and write?' The inquiry did, of course, yield some evidence about the literacy attainments of Year 2 pupils and this is reported in Section 5.

The questionnaire survey

Between October and November 1990 headteachers of 122 nationally representative maintained schools in England and Wales completed a brief questionnaire giving mostly statistical information about their school. Appendix 1 gives details of both the sample and the levels of response. The questionnaire covered such matters as the numbers of pupils and teachers, the types of grouping adopted and the general approach to the teaching of reading. Information derived from this form was used to select a sample of schools for involvement in the case study phase.

In each school, the class teacher of Year 2 (or, in schools with two or more forms of entry, one nominated internally) filled in a substantial teacher enquiry form, providing information under five main headings: teaching styles and strategies; national curriculum; assessment and record keeping; trends; and general information about the class group and the teacher's background. The teacher additionally completed up to ten pupil literacy profiles for individual children in her class, selected by taking alternate names from the register up to a maximum of ten. One hundred and fifteen teachers completed the teacher enquiry form and 754 pupils completed the pupil literacy profile. The pupil literacy profile sought information on pupils' background, their attainment in reading and writing, their attitudes and influences outside school. Details of the profile are given in Appendix 2.

In addition to completing the profile, teachers were asked to provide a sample of the pupil's writing, produced unaided within the previous fortnight. Teachers also provided their assessment of the pupil's performance as a writer on a five-point scale.

The case studies

Between January and July 1991, a subsample of 26 schools, representing five participating LEAs, were visited by a member of the research team, for between half and one complete school day. During this period the researcher spent between one and three hours in the class and a further hour (either in one sitting or split between various points in the session) interviewing the teacher.

The aim of these visits was to carry out in-depth studies: for example, to observe how various methods were put into practice and to follow up issues touched on in the teacher enquiry form. Questions covered systematically in interviews with teachers are listed in Appendix 3.

The brevity of visits should be taken into account when reviewing the descriptions of the schools. A visit of even one day falls short of a thorough 'case study', and the lessons observed could only give a snapshot impression of approaches adopted in any one school. One morning or afternoon may have been atypically influenced by, for example, the numbers of children present, the number of support staff or parents available, teacher illness or even the weather.

Analysis of pupils' writing

In conjunction with the questionnaire survey, samples of pupils' writing were submitted by teachers along with assessments on a five-point scale. Analyses were carried out, not only to establish the characteristics of pupils' writing, but also to relate these to performance levels and to information available from the pupil literacy profile. A discussion of the results of the analyses has particular implications for interpretation of the National Curriculum Attainment Targets, as well as for classroom practice and in-service training. The section has therefore been written and illustrated with pupils' scripts drawn from one authority, in a format that would allow for its use in in-service training; for this reason, the discussion is not integrated into the body of the report but included as Appendix 4.

2. THE SCHOOLS, THE TEACHERS AND THE PUPILS

Questions addressed to headteachers were designed to elicit only such information as was needed for the selection of the case study schools. However, responses from headteachers gave essential background information, for example on the number of pupils and teachers in the school, the types of groupings adopted and the general approach to the teaching of reading. This information was subsequently extended and elaborated by the comments of both teachers and pupils and provides a necessary context for the discussion of the survey results.

2.1 The Survey Schools

Information was received from 122 headteachers. The largest single type of school taking part in the survey - representing nearly half the sample - was the junior and infant school. Only 11 per cent of schools taught infants only. Most schools contained between 100 and 300 children, a quarter of them having 150-200, but both very large (up to 750 pupils) and very small schools, including village schools (less than 50) were also represented.

All of the schools felt able to categorise themselves in general terms of social class of intake. Nineteen per cent described their catchment as middle-class, 34 per cent as working-class, and 38 per cent as a balance between the two. A further eight per cent chose to categorise their families as deprived, unemployed and single-parent, or stressed their multiracial intake.

In organising pupils for learning in school the most common form of grouping was by age, and here a correlation tended to be found between the smallest schools and those employing vertical, or family-grouping. About 29 per cent of schools used both systems, typically moving from family grouping in the infant school to age-grouping in the juniors. Within the class, the predominant method of grouping for learning was by ability (61 per cent), although a quarter of the schools refrained from using any grouping system at all.

Language policies

Over half of the schools (58 per cent) had written their own guidelines on language policy. A further 16 per cent supplemented such guidelines with advice from the LEA. Perhaps surprisingly, only four schools out of the total claimed that their policy consisted of the National Curriculum Programmes of Study, although in later conversation with teachers in the case study schools it became clear that many schools were in the process of rewriting their own guidelines to conform to the National Curriculum.

Among schools visited there was only one with no whole-school policy for the curriculum, and a further three with no policy for language, although in one of these the interviewee asserted that all staff members carried the school's policy 'in their minds'. In all four, the drafting of a language statement was being given a high priority.

Most teachers interviewed felt that in the light of the National Curriculum, their school's policy had become obsolete, and indeed in most cases it was currently being rewritten. This was proving difficult to accomplish in schools with a high turnover of teachers. Previous policies had in many cases been written several years beforehand, by the language coordinator or head, in conjunction with the staff. The writing of such policies, as indeed the rewriting that was taking place currently, had provided a focus for language-based discussion, but where this had happened a long time ago, the policy had become rather remote from teachers' concerns. Most obviously, where the original language coordinator had left, the rest of the staff felt they did not have 'ownership' of their policy. Occasionally, the status of the language policy revealed a rift between the philosophies of the head or language coordinator and the rest of the staff.

Many teachers said they were unclear about the date of development of the policy or of what it consisted. Whether they followed their own strategy or the implied one of the school, the written document itself seemed to have little impact on their practice. In a few cases, parts of it were used selectively, such as a reading inventory or handwriting guidelines.

Teachers were also unsure in most cases as to when their policy had last been used as a focus for staff INSET or discussion: otherwise, unless language had been given special attention, the last relevant staff meeting was given as taking place one or two terms ago. Where the teachers were experienced, it was felt that they were fully conversant with the policy and that, since it had originally received whole-school agreement, there was no further need for discussion. New teachers tended to be given a copy of it as part of their induction.

Among the survey schools methods of communicating to parents the school's reading and writing policy were diverse, varying from an open-door policy, practical demonstrations and parent workshops to communicating test results, or in one instance, even advising parents not to teach reading at home. Once again, schools usually communicated with parents by more than one means. Most frequent was transmitting some information about the home-school liaison programme (34 per cent), and circulating brochures or sheets on reading policy.

While the majority of headteachers provided parents with some kind of information about the teaching of reading, only one in ten specifically mentioned their communication of a writing policy. Often, this was a style sheet on the handwriting script taught in the school. Clearly in this area there is markedly less liaison with parents than in that concerning reading.

Pupils with special needs

Given the cross-section of schools taking part in this study, ranging from two-teacher village schools to those in inner-city areas, the numbers of pupils with special educational needs (SEN) and with English as a second language (ESL) in each class varied greatly. Some teachers interviewed seemed unclear as to the number and kinds of languages spoken amongst their pupils and there was also some confusion of the terms 'English as a second language' and 'bilingual'. As regards SEN, teachers' knowledge about their pupils' problems varied in specificity from a detailed list of symptoms to a generalised definition of 'poor ability'. SEN embraced both learning and behavioural difficulties, the two often being elided, both in the school's perception and in the psychologist's requirements for statementing.

Most teachers in schools visited found the amount of support available for either SEN or ESL children inadequate. Time allocations from a specially-trained teacher varied: in one school, the single statemented child had a full-time ancillary helper allocated to her, in another no help was available from the LEA despite 70 out of a total of 300 pupils being statemented. More typically, the four or five relevant children were receiving the equivalent of approximately half a day's special tuition per week. Teachers often commented that the majority of their pupils with learning or behavioural difficulties were not even in the statementing process: these children could, in teachers' estimates, outnumber those statemented by a ratio of 5:1.

Despite outside help being more commonly available for SEN than for ESL pupils, teachers nonetheless had almost no expectations of support from their education authority. There was an almost universal disbelief in the process of statementing, which seemed to be undertaken only in order to procure remedial support. One teacher felt that, even if the 'struggle' of the statementing process succeeded, the trouble involved in going through it would not be worth the small amount of help that would be forthcoming as a result. Statementing was held to label the child prematurely, so that many teachers would not contemplate it for this reason alone; others were entirely cynical about the prospect of almost any child being accepted for statementing. One school limited itself to submitting only the most extreme cases so as to raise their chances of success. The lengthiness of the process, and the very infrequent visits of the educational psychologist, were also given as reasons why children were not entered for statementing. Some teachers were torn also between recognising that such pupils needed withdrawal, and wanting them to mix with and benefit from learning with other pupils in the mainstream.

2.2 The Teachers in the Survey Schools

Headteachers in most of the survey schools reported a stable situation with regard to staffing; only 12 per cent considered they had experienced problems with the turnover of teachers.

Three-quarters of the 115 Year 2 teachers completing the teacher enquiry form had been trained specifically to teach infants; an overlapping 60 per cent had received junior training. Only seven per cent had come from a secondary school background and had not received any infant-level initial teacher training. A substantial majority of teachers (83 per cent) had taught age-groups other than infant; of these, 72 per cent had taught juniors, and 13 per cent secondary ages. Under two per cent described themselves as having taught all age-groups.

Some participants held one or more positions of responsibility within their school. Most frequent, at 27 per cent, were language coordinators; and second (21 per cent), infant school heads or team leaders.

Views on reading skills

When teachers were interviewed they were asked to describe the main skills in reading that they wanted their pupils to acquire. With the exception of a couple of teachers who had difficulty answering this question, concentrating on their approaches rather than the aims that lay behind them, all of them gave responses that fell into two clear categories. Most commonly - and despite the wording of the question that emphasised 'skills' - teachers stressed their wish for the pupils to develop a love of books, and an enjoyment of reading - both characteristics that referred to the child's self-concept as a reader. Fluency was also given high priority. Secondly, a somewhat smaller group listed skills such as word-building or decoding. A few teachers gave both categories of answer, usually but not always in the order of priority described here.

Views on language and language teaching

Teachers interviewed were also asked to what extent their teaching of reading was associated with their teaching of writing and talking. This proved to be a very difficult question for them to answer. Most responses fell into two categories: either asserting in general terms that 'it's all language, really', that all three were 'totally intertwined' or 'very much interconnected'; or citing examples of work they had undertaken where a piece of writing had led to discussion, or some reading to writing. Sometimes the examples given were rather divorced from the issue in hand: for example, one teacher (a language coordinator) referred to the way she tried to get her pupils to 'speak in sentences'. Several teachers stressed how all subjects depended on language, although their priorities amongst the three modes varied: some highlighting speaking, some reading and some writing. Only one teacher said she taught reading and writing separately, because each child had a different level of performance in each; and one other further complained that her pupils could not see the link between the two, as evidenced by their inability to read their own writing or her words on the classroom walls.

In a related question, teachers were also asked to what extent their own view of language affected their teaching of other subjects or curriculum areas. If anything, this question proved even harder to answer than the one above. It frequently had to be rephrased, for example, to ask specifically whether they would expect the same kind of writing from, for example, a story and a science report. A sizeable group of teachers asserted that all subjects posed the same kind of language demands in terms of reading and writing. Reporting was 'just a different kind of writing'. Many others explained their different expectations of scientific writing. Interestingly, teachers' attitudes in this regard were often in striking contrast to one another. The technical vocabulary that was integral to science was held by some to require accurate spelling (and neat handwriting), while others thought that lenient standards of accuracy should be permitted. Scientific writing was rarely described in terms of formal differences from narrative (indeed, one teacher likened it to 'news' in being chronological). Rather, it was seen as demanding proper sentences, good presentation and descriptive words. One interviewee said she wanted the children to 'put something exciting' into science writing, and to avoid the 'ands' which would be acceptable in a story as long as the events were in the right sequence.

A few teachers commented more vigorously on the need for different styles of writing to suit different purposes and audiences. Science and related subjects (such as cooking) could be exploited for their potential to respond flexibly - a recipe could be outlined in pictures, not prose, for example. Science, one said, was useful for teaching the use of lists and the description of processes, and history for learning 'sequencing and progression'. Overall, and particularly in the light of National Curriculum requirements for English, teachers' lack of awareness of the different language demands of areas of the curriculum was worthy of note.

2.3 Pupils in the Survey Schools

Background information on the pupils taking part in the survey was derived both from teachers and from the pupil literacy profiles, completed by 754 pupils.

Pre-school exposure to reading and writing

One part of the pupil literacy profile required teachers to classify pupils according to five categories of reading attainment: fluent (beyond their age); competent; emergent, early reader; almost ready to read; pre-reader. Teachers were also asked to say whether the children concerned could read before they came to school. Approximately ten per cent of them had been able to do so, including just over a third of the children who were classified as fluent readers. The teachers were also asked to say whether the children could write their names before coming to school. Approximately four out of ten had been able to do so and 16 per cent had been able to write other recognisable words or sentences. However, the information requested about children's reading and writing before school was not available or known to their teacher in a third of the cases. Other evidence relating to how the children were taught to read suggests that the number of children who had, in their own opinion, learnt to read at home was greater than some teachers in Year 2 believed.

When, for example, the children were asked how they had learned to read, 44 per cent referred to the person who had taught them. Of these the largest category (22 per cent) said that they had been taught to read by their mother, 16 per cent referred to the teacher and six per cent to another member of their family.

Influences on reading and writing performance

Over 80 per cent of the children said that grown-ups sometimes read with them at home or listened to them reading. Just under 70 per cent said that grown-ups sometimes took them to the library. However, a quarter of the fluent readers and four out of ten of the non-readers indicated that they were never taken to a library. Almost all children (95 per cent) said they had books of their own at home, although six per cent of the non-readers said that they had no books. Parents are not the only people at home involved in the children's education. No less than 38 per cent of the pupils said that a brother or sister read with them at home, and in eight per cent of cases grandparents did the same.

Responses indicated that parents were less likely to be involved in the teaching of writing than reading. About 60 per cent of the pupils said that someone at home sometimes wrote with them; but for a third of pupils this did not happen. As other research studies have found, early instruction in writing, whether or not the pupils were able to write recognisable words or sentences before starting school, related very significantly to reported performance in both reading and writing.

There was a highly significant association between reported performance in reading and the degree of active interest shown by parents. Just under 80 per cent of the parents were said to have an active interest in their child's education. This was more likely to be the case for fluent readers (87 per cent) than for non-readers (58 per cent) and for good writers (85 per cent) as opposed to non-writers (50 per cent).

Teachers were asked to outline any personal or social factors, or home or school circumstances, that might have affected a child's success or difficulties with reading or writing. Of those who completed the question the largest proportion referred to family circumstances. Just under half of those responding (46 per cent) referred to home conditions which had adversely affected performance. Twenty-eight per cent referred to home conditions that had assisted pupils. The next most frequent category (17 per cent) referred to pupils' behavioural difficulties. Ten per cent mentioned the fact that English was not the pupils' first language.

It was possible to investigate the strength of the associations between certain of the background factors about which information was obtained and the reported literacy attainments of the pupils. Children were more likely to be classified as fluent or competent readers if their fathers had paid employment (54 per cent as opposed to 33 per cent), if the family owned its own home (63 per cent as opposed to 33 per cent), and if the child did not have to share a room (55 per cent as opposed to 41 per cent). If, however, the child had a television in his or her room, as one in five pupils had, there was less likelihood of being classified as a good reader (35 per cent as opposed to 52 per cent).

Attitudes to reading, writing and television

One section of the pupil literacy profile invited pupils to indicate the feelings they associated with reading, writing and watching television, in relation to a five-point scale. The scale consisted of symbols representing an expression of pleasure at one extreme, and of displeasure at the other.

Nearly all pupils enjoyed reading and being read to. Information obtained from the headteacher and teacher questionnaires suggested that most headteachers and class teachers would regard such enjoyment on the part of their pupils as one of their main objectives in reading instruction. In this particular respect, schools appear to be very successful in achieving their aims.

Writing was somewhat less popular than reading. Seventy-five per cent of the pupils indicated that they liked reading very much, whereas just over 55 per cent liked writing very much. Forty per cent indicated that they found it difficult to read and write. The main reasons given were to the effect that some words were hard to read or to spell. In general, however, their answers indicated that, despite the difficulties they were conscious of, most children enjoyed reading and writing.

Children were also asked what they liked or disliked about writing, and what constituted good writing. Good stories were held to be long ones, written by pupils who first thought about what they were going to say, and who persevered until the task was completed. Those describing themselves as good writers also felt themselves to be fast writers and good spellers, able to tackle more than just the 'easy' words on display on the walls. Children from a school with a policy of emergent writing felt that plot construction was no harder than the secretarial aspects such as spelling and handwriting, although a concentration on the latter was more common. One child said she disliked writing because 'it made her hand and brain ache'.

The fuller analysis in Appendix 4 of children's writing, and children's attitudes to writing, as these were expressed in the pupil literacy profiles, shows that they tended to focus attention on matters to do with aspects of spelling and handwriting (ATs 4 and 5). From work with older children it has been found that such a focus of attention on surface features of writing is the norm rather than the exception. Given this situation, it is suggested that teachers should be concerned to monitor the extent to which pupils' perceptions about writing expand with their competence as communicators. Concerns about the content, form and style of what is written also need consideration, even when children are at the earliest stages of learning to communicate in writing.

Just under nine out of ten pupils across all the survey schools indicated that they enjoyed watching television and most of these (65 per cent) said that they liked doing it very much. Fourteen per cent of the pupils watched television for four hours or more a day. Of these, over half normally watched television till bedtime. Eight out of ten children said that they also had a video recorder at home.

3. PROVISION, ORGANISATION AND USE OF RESOURCES

3.1 School and Classroom Libraries

Virtually all schools had a school library, generally housed in a separate room, and 59 per cent of these contained over 1000 books. One in five held fewer than 400. The disparity of resources in this respect was evident, but of course is related to the size of the school. The quantity of books held in the school library is not, however, in itself an indicator of the book resources available to pupils and teachers. In most schools (84 per cent), all classrooms also had a book corner.

In nine out of ten schools, the policy was that pupils were permitted to take books home. It appeared usual for pupils to take home, on a daily or weekly basis, their reading book plus a library book. The latter might be for an adult to read to the child. When asked about the arrangements for borrowing and using library books, however, a third of responding classteachers said that library books were available for class use only. In a minority of schools the home-borrowing scheme was being reviewed since it had resulted in the loss of many books.

When using the library for work across the curriculum, teachers interviewed said they selected books for topic work, or asked pupils to do this for them, and often supplemented home resources with project packs from the public library or schools library service. In no school did a teacher mention using information or other books to develop reference or study skills, or to look at different genres of text.

Class libraries in schools visited, unlike school libraries, tended to carry a predominance of fiction. However, even in schools that espoused an approach involving the use of 'real books', the numbers of books available could be remarkably few. Fifty to seventy books in a class library was not uncommon. The numbers of non-fiction, reference and poetry books were also highly variable, some classes possessing perhaps only half a dozen of these.

Class libraries, or book corners, operated a rudimentary form of classification in separating fiction from non-fiction books. Information books themselves could be undifferentiated, or grouped according to 'curriculum subject' (Science, Nature, The World, etc.) or according to vaguer definitions such as 'People who help us', or even 'Books we like to read' and 'More books to enjoy'. Subject classification was seen by some teachers to be a big hurdle for seven-year-olds. Nonetheless, whilst some teachers left children to infer the layout of the class library, others deliberately explained the system at the beginning of the school year.

Whilst the colour-coding by topic was more typical of the non-fiction books held in the school library, fiction in the class was frequently colour-banded. This was also found in some schools that openly subscribed to a 'real books' approach, and there was some evidence of a move back to colour-coding in schools that had previously attempted non-categorised systems. In these schools it appeared that teachers felt the need for some structure, and believed that children benefited from it too: otherwise it was thought children could become demoralised by choosing books that were inappropriate to their abilities. It must be said that the reverse view was also expressed: that children would learn from their mistakes, and that parents would always be available to help with a difficult book.

In some classes, the subdivision of books into fiction and non-fiction, or into levels of difficulty, had broken down. All that remained were measures such as grouping 'big books on the bottom and small ones on the top'. Reading schemes tended to be the most clearly grouped, in boxes according to level.

Children in the schools visited seemed mostly unaware of any principle of organisation in their class book corner, regardless of whether it had one or not. However, they seemed unperturbed by this, generally relying on judging books by their cover in order to make a selection. They were in agreement that easy books had pictures and large print, although some could look like 'baby books' but be harder because of the small print size.

Whilst they seemed to prefer 'real' to scheme fiction, and fiction to information books, almost no child showed any awareness of book titles or authors. When a book was referred to specifically, it tended to be part of a scheme and to be described by its colour or level banding, or just by its series name (New Way, Nippers, etc.). Real books and scheme books were differentiated as 'single' or 'library' books which could be taken home, and 'sets of books' which usually could not. Progress in reading was generally perceived in terms of moving from one level or colour of a scheme to the next.

Children rarely seemed to be entrusted with responsibility for keeping their class library in good order. Tidying up tended to happen at the end of a day, a week, or just when matters got out of hand, although a few teachers appointed monitors in rotation. In most schools the teacher had to finish the job of clearing up that the children had started. Where volunteers were recruited on an ad hoc basis they almost invariably were girls. Class book corners varied radically in the degree of order they presented, and in clarity of layout and general attractiveness.

3.2 Use of Tape Recorders and Information Technology

Tape recorders appeared not to be in much use in the classes visited. In a few classrooms they were permanently stationed on a table for easy access by the pupils. In others they were partially available, kept in a cupboard to be drawn on for specific activities. Again, one or two teachers expressed overt dislike of this form of technology ('Personally, I loathe them') but most were making use of it, finding it especially useful for lower-ability pupils or for those with English as a second language. Strategies, for all abilities, included: listening to story-tapes (sometimes followed by writing in which the format would be changed); taping records of class visits; exchanging taped letters with penfriend schools; and interviewing classmates or adults.

In discussions about their use of information technology, what was most striking was the teachers' lack of confidence and, in most cases, the lack of awareness of its potential. This was often accompanied by feelings of antipathy: one called the computer 'a pain in the neck'; it was 'just another thing for recording or feeding in data, if you could bear the boredom'. Another described it as time-consuming because of the necessity of sitting with the children whilst they worked. In some schools, children had been trained to operate the computer by themselves, often following written instructions, and indeed this autonomy was prized by their teachers as one of IT's advantages.

Whilst some teachers only used the computer for language games (useful because attention-retaining), those employing wordprocessing seldom used it in the way recommended by the National Curriculum. As a tool for writing development, the wordprocessor, with its facilities for reshaping text so easily, is eminently suited. Teachers typically used it for the 'fair-copying' of completed, pencil-written texts. Redrafting (and the word itself was not necessarily used with the children) seemed to be interpreted as a method of correcting the spellings on work typed up on screen.

The advantage of the computer was seen primarily in terms of novelty. Were it not for the necessity of chidren learning to handle the tools of the modern world, they might as well have been using pencils. Its other benefit was in producing neat work, both on screen and in printout, in which mistakes could be painlessly rectified. The clarity of the screen meant that attention could easily be drawn to points of spelling, punctuation or grammar. Whilst two teachers said that wordprocessing was inappropriate for six-year-olds who needed to practise their handwriting, others valued the high status that print gave to children's work in their own eyes. Of course by implication it downgraded their own handwriting.

Only about three of the 26 teachers were overtly aware of the potential benefits of wordprocessing in the language curriculum and the enhancement of reading skills and oral communication that could result from the use of good programs. The teachers showing such awareness and enthusiasm had had specialised IT training, and, in their classes, the computer was always available for use and always in demand.

Both with regard to IT and tape recorders, it seemed that where the teacher was enthusiastic about the medium, positive use was made of it.

3.3 Classroom Support

Twelve of the 26 teachers in schools visited received no teaching assistance. One had the equivalent of a full-time assistant, and received assistance for half a week. The rest received help ranging from three hours to three mornings a week. One teacher, with a class of 32 pupils, 11 of whom spoke English as a second language, and the majority of whom came late on the day of the visit, received assistance only on an irregular basis.

Many pupils had the opportunity to read about once a week to a visitor: for example, a parent, student, governor, non-teaching assistant or nursery nurse. Seventy-three per cent of teachers completing the enquiry form confirmed that they had the assistance of another adult in class on a regular basis. Help on a daily basis, however, was available in only one in five of the survey schools. Although the practice of using helpers was quite widespread there remained several teachers who voiced a concern at delegating even partial responsibility for the hearing of reading to non-professional outsiders, fearing that problems would go unnoticed. It seemed that they were reluctant to delegate any part of what was seen to be one of their key obligations. It was apparently perceived to be such by parents.

Among the survey schools 91 per cent of those with a 'middle-class' intake had a home-school scheme as opposed to 76 per cent of schools in 'working-class' areas. When asked whether they had the opportunity to involve parents in their classroom activities, for either reading or writing, most teachers (77 per cent) said that this was possible. However, 20 per cent said that they did not have the opportunity to do so. Parental involvement in school varied enormously in degree, from the occasional visit by one of a number of 'floating' volunteers, to daily visits by regulars, some of whom were themselves teachers taking time out to bring up their own children.

The majority of teachers also organised some form of scheme which involved parental participation in reading or writing instruction at home. In most instances, this involved reading or book-sharing. Other aspects of language development, for example, involving writing or spelling, were relatively uncommon (referred to by five per cent of teachers). Schools which had parental participation in class were more likely to have home-school schemes operating also. Figures for both in practice were high: 83 per cent of schools involved parents at school in some capacity, and 87 per cent at home.

Teachers completing the enquiry form were asked also to say what provision, if any, was made for children with reading difficulties, either within the resources allocated to the school or available from the LEA. In schools, assistance was given in some cases by a language support or special needs teacher (27 per cent) or by a part-time teacher (21 per cent). In 15 per cent of cases, teachers said that the pupil would be given individual help or extra help in a small group. At LEA level, assistance was provided by the school psychologists (23 per cent) or a teacher working for a special needs or remedial service (17 per cent). In some cases (16 per cent) such assistance was provided for statemented children only. Four out of ten teachers reported no LEA assistance for their pupils. Some of those explicitly stated that LEA policy was to provide support for junior pupils only.

4. CLASSROOM PRACTICE

4.1 Classroom Management

Enquiries in the schools visited suggested that class size, whether large or small, appeared to have little influence on the way teachers organised pupils. Since the great majority of teachers organised pupils into groups for most learning activities, large classes merely resulted in more groups. There was a tendency, however, for teachers of large classes to favour formal class teaching or activities which could be carried out by pupils independently. There was also less opportunity to hear individual pupils read in large classes.

Although some teachers were influenced by the size and layout of the classroom, organisational strategies depended in most cases on the content of the lessons, and decisions about grouping were dictated as much by management concerns as by pedagogical principles. Among teachers in the schools visited, only two used whole-class teaching as their main strategy, while others adopted this approach only for handwriting, class discussions, and, on occasion, for story writing. Groups were formed either according to social criteria or by ability. In the latter case it was more usually mathematical or general ability that guided the teacher's choices, rarely language ability.

The use of groups did not necessarily mean that pupils on one table were actively involved in working together. Where ability groups were operating, children were sometimes doing the same work as the rest of the class, but in a different sequence. Language work, especially, tended not only to be introduced collectively but to be the same for all abilities, with different levels of achievement being expected. Most teachers stressed that their groups were flexible, and could be changed termly, weekly and even daily. Several teachers used both social and ability groupings at different times, depending on the work being carried out, with social groups being used typically for practical, 'non-academic' subjects such as art or construction. In vertically grouped classes, groups tended to be by age. It was apparent that the greater the flexibility of the groups, the greater the need for rigorous record-keeping.

When asked how often they heard each pupil read, teachers interviewed responded with rates that varied from 'every day' to 'once a week'. The poorest readers were given priority for daily attention. The less frequent the sessions, the more time they expected to devote to each, although all teachers aimed to hear each child for not less than ten minutes. The need for quality time was stressed. Early readers would tend to read an entire book, fluent ones, given their more substantial books, less. Only one teacher spoke in terms of a number of pages typically read (two). Given that the research team rarely witnessed any child being heard to read, it was difficult to see how teachers fitted the implied 30 to 150 such sessions into their week. Arrangements whereby the more proficient readers 'looked after themselves', such as writing book reviews instead of reading aloud, or reading in pairs (taking a passage from a book in turn) enabled teachers to reduce their assumed burden to manageable proportions.

Another question addressed to teachers was about peer-tutoring. Overall the strategy was not liked, a view apparently shared by parents, since, by analogy with the Victorian system of 'monitors', it was thought to hold the brighter pupils back. One teacher only refrained from using it because she had no pupils able enough to teach the others. This view was sometimes held by those same teachers who employed social groupings, particularly in order to let all children benefit from working with peers either more or less able than themselves. One teacher, though, felt peer-tutoring was useful because it challenged able or older pupils to use their linguistic resources for the purpose of explaining work to the less able. Where used, peer-tutoring took the form of reading pairs instituted by the teacher so as to combine better and poorer readers. Such pairing of infant readers with junior was becoming less frequent owing, it was suggested, to the pressures of the National Curriculum. The system was not at all popular, and one teacher said she did not use it because some pupils felt that shared reading was not 'real work'. Overall, peer-tutoring tended to occur only spontaneously, with children reading together or helping each other with spellings, and not as a result of conscious organisation on the part of the teacher.

Teachers organised reading practice in a variety of ways. Silent reading (USSR: Uninterrupted Sustained Silent Reading) or, more commonly, quiet reading (ERIC: Everybody reads in class), was almost universal. It took place anything from twice a day, for up to 20 minutes, to fortnightly. Forty-four per cent of survey schools reported silent reading on a daily basis. A minority of teachers felt it was inappropriate for children so young, although the high noise content of some observed sessions seemed to be a result more of poor control than of the children's immaturity. While the principle of quiet or silent reading is that everyone, including the teacher, reads (and in one school it happened at the same time across all year groups), this session was sometimes used for catching up with the unending task of listening to pupils read.

Reading pairs - another vehicle for reading practice - were either determined by the teacher, or freely chosen; sometimes both patterns were used. Structured time in which to read to an allocated partner was an infrequent occurrence and reading to a friend tended to happen spontaneously. There was almost no opportunity for Year 2 children in this survey to read to children either older or younger than themselves, although several teachers said this had been customary in the past and that they were hoping to reintroduce it. One of the schools visited had developed its visitor scheme so that each child was paired with a particular adult with whom a relationship could be built up. Pupils had the opportunity to read to adults other than their teacher in 90 per cent of classrooms, and in a majority (67 per cent) they read to each other. Similarly, about two thirds of pupils were given the opportunity to engage in 'book talk' in the absence of the teacher. In over half of classes, children were invited individually to act as a storyteller to the class. Two children reading in unison appeared to be a less common practice (33 per cent).

The results of the questionnaire survey showed that some reading practices that might be conceived of as 'old fashioned' commanded a sizeable number of adherents. Children in a group taking turns to read aloud (39 per cent) or in unison (19 per cent) was broadly as popular a strategy as children taking turns in reading around the class (32 per cent) or reading as a class in unison (23 per cent). While nearly all teachers read to their pupils, about a fifth (19 per cent) also did so when the children were engaged in some other, silent activity, such as sewing. None of this group of reading activities occurred commonly on a daily basis and they appeared to be used only occasionally.

Nevertheless, it should be noted that in the schools visited reading was always available to children on completion of their tasks, even if it was observed to be taken up with varying degrees of enthusiasm. The fact that teachers almost invariably claimed that their children loved reading was not wholly consistent with this observation. One teacher suggested that the pupils read so much in the course of a day's work that they were more likely to pick another activity as a time filler.

A final issue relating to classroom management concerns the organisation of work for SEN pupils. Teachers interviewed were roughly divided in their approaches towards integrating the SEN pupils. Those who grouped them separately, giving them their own work, claimed that this was necessary because behavioural and learning difficulties often went hand in hand. The SEN children were seen as demanding extra time and attention, not least to prevent them disrupting the others' work - a demand that needed to be handled skilfully if the rest of the class was not to suffer. While adopting a segregationist approach, teachers were conscious that SEN pupils might feel inferior to, or ostracised from, other pupils. Some teachers changed the order in which they distributed work to groups so as to disguise the relative rankings of each group.

The strategy of masking SEN pupils' differentness also cropped up in comments from teachers operating, conversely, an integrated approach. In a multi-activity classroom following an integrated day, no pupils were particularly aware of what work the SEN pupils were engaged in. Where they were given the same work, they were set lower level targets. Sometimes they would be paired with those of 'normal' ability for non-academic work such as art or construction in order to let the SEN child lead, while in other cases teachers allocated reading partners of deliberately disparate abilities. The integrationists distributed the SEN children, split up from each other, across their mixed-ability work groups, or kept mainly to classwork in order to spare them the difficulties they experienced in working in groups.

Some teachers used a combination of these two approaches but, regardless of the system adopted, they felt that the SEN pupils required extra time, attention and help from them, and commonly felt guilty about their perceived inability to devise new strategies to move them on. Pupils with special needs enforced changes in teaching styles, reflected in predominantly oral responses to tasks on the part of the teacher, greater assistance with writing, or a stronger focus on practical activities.

4.2 Teaching Methods

Teaching reading

In view of the recurrent debate about the use of 'real books', it must first of all be pointed out that only four per cent of headteachers taking part in the survey claimed their schools exclusively used 'real books' in teaching reading. This replicates the findings of Her Majesty's Inspectorate (DES, 1990). Much more common, conversely, was an exclusive reliance on one or more reading schemes (together, 28 per cent). However, the most usual approach (nearly 67 per cent of schools) was to combine the use of 'real books' and reading schemes.

Headteachers were asked to explain how they would describe the school's approach to reading instruction to an interested parent. When categorised into themes, their answers fell into three types: the general (e.g. 'holistic approach', lots of reading); the skill-based specific (methods such as phonics, or teaching basic sight vocabulary); and the 'child-centred' (promoting enjoyment/ confidence). Most heads listed several aspects in describing their overall approach, and the first category (generalised reading approach) was mentioned most often. Within this category, the adoption of a broad approach and a variety of practices was cited most frequently (mentioned by 27 per cent of heads). One in three heads mentioned the use of structured methods. Over a third of headteachers mentioned the importance of parental involvement, and most of these further stressed that responsibility for reading progress was shared between school and home.

Teachers were also asked to describe their approach to reading instruction, and their responses are illustrated in Figure 4.1, below. Five per cent of the class teachers responding to the enquiry form said that they used an approach involving 'real books' exclusively, thus corroborating the evidence provided by headteachers. Eighty-three per cent of teachers said that they used a combination of reading schemes and 'real books', a substantially higher proportion than was reported by headteachers. More class teachers than headteachers described their school as using a combination of approaches; similarly, in a number of schools, the heads described their approach as one based on several reading schemes, whilst the teachers claimed that 'real books' were also used.

Figure 4.1 Materials used to teach reading

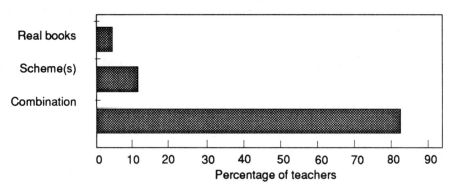

In describing their methods of teaching reading, as opposed to materials used, almost all teachers reported that they used what was termed a 'phonic' approach and just over a quarter of the sample (26 per cent) used this method most often in their teaching. Nine out of ten teachers reported that they used a method of teaching involving 'Look and Say' and a fifth said this was the method they used most frequently. Figure 4.2 illustrates the extent to which different methods were used.

Figure 4.2 Methods of teaching reading

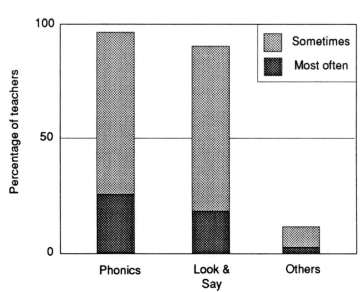

Twelve per cent of the teachers used other methods, but few (three per cent) used these as the predominant method of teaching. Those referred to included, in order of frequency, the use of reading schemes or programmes such as 'Breakthrough to Literacy' or 'Letterland'; an approach involving the use of 'real books' only (also referred to by teachers as a storybook or apprenticeship approach); or an approach involving shared reading.

In addition to these strategies, numerous other reading and writing practices and activities were employed by teachers. Over half (55 per cent), for example, said that they listened to individual pupils reading on a daily basis. The others listened to reading, but less frequently. In just over half of the schools (52 per cent), teachers read to the class on a daily basis.

There was general agreement among teachers interviewed about combining phonic and whole word (Look and Say) approaches, selected to suit the context and the individual child. Look and Say methods tended to be used for beginning readers only, and hence were falling out of use by Year 2. However, word lists around the classroom obviously acted as a Look and Say resource for reading and writing. In view of the recent controversy on the issue, it should be noted that no teacher disclaimed the use of phonics. Most teachers thought phonics necessary for all children and some regarded it as particularly necessary for children 'falling behind'.

Teachers varied substantially in their use of phonics, and in how systematic this use was. It was those teachers most wedded to a particular reading scheme who tended to believe most strongly in the gradual introduction of a controlled vocabulary. Some only taught phonic points to individual children as the need arose; some assembled small groups experiencing the same problem in order to 'trouble-shoot'; others taught 'a sound a week' to the whole class whether all children needed it or not. This last approach might well take the form of a game. Of course, a number of teachers were using all three of these approaches to phonics, along with the judicious use of Look and Say, apparently guided very much by intuition rather than any set of formalised procedures.

Teaching writing

When asked in an open question to describe their approach to writing, teachers gave answers which fell into two broad categories: those referring, respectively, to the secretarial and the composing aspects of the writing process. As regards secretarial skills, teachers stressed the importance of good handwriting (32 per cent) and accurate spelling and punctuation (12 per cent); and furthermore listed a range of 'mechanical' writing activities they employed. These were the use of dictionaries or word books (29 per cent), copying (18 per cent), the teacher acting as scribe (19 per cent), and 'sentence building' (10 per cent).

Compositional approaches themselves appeared to subdivide into three aspects. The first stressed writing for different purposes and audiences, or in different styles (21 per cent for each of these comments). The second cited a range of open-ended techniques for writing, most commonly using pre-writing activities (18 per cent) or shared writing (10 per cent), with redrafting, using talk or stories to stimulate writing, and having a writing corner also being mentioned (together 11 per cent). The third, and most substantial, group of compositional approaches could be termed the developmental. This approach emphasised the need for child-centredness. Creativity and risk-taking had to be encouraged, as also did writing from one's own experience (15 per cent each). A policy of emergent writing was followed (12 per cent), with the child working at his or her own pace (five per cent), allowed independence (12 per cent) and suitably motivated (nine per cent). Twelve per cent of teachers also associated their teaching of writing specifically with phonics work.

It became clear during visits to schools that class teachers were commonly employing a much wider range of tactics and activities in teaching reading and writing than they gave themselves credit for in describing their practice. Whilst they seemed to experience some difficulty in articulating both their methods and the view of language that underlay their choice of them, their classroom practice itself often reflected a greater variety of techniques than they had specified on the questionnaire or in the interview.

4.3 Monitoring and Assessment

A large proportion of teachers in the survey schools (60 per cent) made use of screening tests or assessments to gauge reading attainment. Less than a third (29 per cent) of those using tests did so for diagnostic purposes. Listening to pupils reading was the most common method used to assess pupils by informal methods (80 per cent of teachers cited this). A minority (28 per cent) referred to the use of a form of miscue analysis, while a large number mentioned the use of some form of assessment of 'comprehension' (55 per cent).

In the event of new pupils arriving in class, teachers used a wide variety of methods for establishing how to begin reading instruction. These ranged from reference to relevant records (mentioned by 37 per cent of teachers) to talk with the pupil about reading (34 per cent). The use of miscue analysis (31 per cent) was also referred to, as was the use of available reading materials to establish a general level of performance, or the uncontrolled selection of a book by the pupil concerned (25 per cent). Other forms of informal assessment were used by a substantial minority of teachers (23 per cent).

It is worth noting that almost no helper in the classes visited, except the professionals (SEN peripatetic, Travellers' support), kept written records of work done or problems encountered. Instead they would communicate with the class teacher orally. The class teachers felt, almost unanimously, that this strategy was adequate, especially since the helper was working in the same room and could be observed. The work produced by the child was said to act as a record. Further records were considered unnecessary because the helpers did work that had been allocated by the teacher.

Despite the introduction of Standard Assessment Tasks, the use of existing tests did not appear to be phased out. However, almost all class teachers expressed a dislike of and disbelief in the efficacy of formal testing, a view which appeared to predate the introduction of National Curriculum Assessment. It was held to be 'of no benefit to anyone', being able to 'give you half an hour of silence but not tell you anything'. Such teachers questioned how often the results were helpful, beyond their use in 'covering' the class teacher and in informing other agencies. Some group or individual reading tests in use were seen as being ill-matched to current conceptions of reading or to the requirements of the National Curriculum, and only needed for diagnosis or remedial purposes. Whilst such tests tended to be administered as school policy by the headteacher, sometimes without the class teacher's understanding or cooperation, the latter typically felt that formal assessment was not needed if the teacher knew the pupils well. The assumption was that the teacher's professionalism was sufficient to identify failure on a day-to-day basis.

Informal assessment was much more common. Some LEAs required the completion of their own record sheets and all teachers operated some system of reading record books or cards. The degree of detail which these provided varied, from a simple note of the date and title of book read, to detailed observational comments. Only one of the 26 case-study teachers refused to show her record book to the researcher. Many schools were also operating home-school contact books (although such schemes, usually started in Reception, could be waning in popularity two years later), keeping samples of work, or doing miscue analyses. For many teachers, the process of assessment was intuitive: 'It just comes with experience, you know where your children are'.

Again citing professional intuition, teachers had great difficulty in describing how they ensured that progress in reading occurred. For one, it was a 'horrendous' process of fortnightly weekend reviews and planning, 'burning the midnight oil'. Teachers' responses to this issue divided broadly into what might be called the mechanical and the holistic. In the first group were answers that concentrated on tactics such as hearing the child read more, changing to a different book/scheme, questioning the parents, investigating possible physical problems and so on. Knowing the level in the scheme the child had reached, or the number of ticks on a list of Attainment Targets, was sometimes held by this group to be a guide to progress. From the second group came responses relating to knowing the individual child well, so that appropriate help could be formulated. It involved regularly reviewing progress, usually by conferring with the child, and keeping detailed records.

4.4 Impact of the National Curriculum

Teachers were asked to indicate on the enquiry form what new practices in reading and writing instruction they had introduced as a result of the National Curriculum. Such new practices tended to involve writing rather than reading; for example, teachers had introduced more varied writing styles and more work on punctuation and spelling.

In response to a question about the introduction of new materials, however, the most frequent categories of response referred to the use of a greater variety of reading materials (11 per cent) and the greater use of 'real books' (10 per cent) as a teaching resource. This is presumably in response to the statutory requirement that pupils should be exposed to 'a range of rich and stimulating texts'. Conversely, some teachers (seven per cent) said that the introduction of the National Curriculum had meant that they had less time for listening to children reading and for giving instruction relating to phonics or spelling (three per cent). Whilst this was a problem experienced most acutely during the three weeks of Standard Assessment Tasks administration in 1991, it was also a feature of normal classroom life. When asked specifically about language activities that may have been curtailed, 16 per cent of the teachers said that they had less time for reading with pupils and for listening to reading. Ten per cent said that they had less time for non-theme-related reading and discussion.

Teachers interviewed elaborated on the difficulty they had in finding time to listen to children read and several said that they were now forced to hear reading outside class time: in lunchtime, breaks, before school or during assembly. One managed to get through her entire class three times a week on lunchtimes only, by taking all (ten) boys on Mondays and again on Wednesdays, all (20) girls on Tuesdays and Thursdays, and the whole class on Friday afternoon. Significantly, she found that, being better readers, the larger number of girls could be processed in the same amount of time as required by the boys.

Teachers were asked in the course of the survey to indicate from a list of textual resources recommended by the National Curriculum those which they usually had on display or readily available in their classroom. Each category was well represented, especially posters (90 per cent), notices (96 per cent) and labels (98 per cent). Least common were directories (25 per cent), menus (30 per cent), and texts in other languages (21 per cent).

A substantial minority of teachers interviewed claimed that the National Curriculum had made no difference to the way they taught reading and writing, either because they had always taught in the way it prescribed, or because they were not going to let it change their traditional style. For some, it had had a burdensome effect, involving additional elements to those they had always included. Another response was to curtail projects relating to the topics assessed, once enough evidence had been accumulated to 'tick off' the relevant Attainment Targets, even though they might otherwise have been continued in response to pupils' enthusiasm.

Where teachers cited specific ways in which the National Curriculum had influenced language work, these took many forms. A few said they were now more aware of what they were listening for in children's talk, or looking for in their writing. Indeed, it had made them more observant of their own speech and writing. Whilst one teacher appreciated the new focus on skills in preference to knowledge, most teachers expressed reservations about aspects which they felt now to be stressed. Formal spelling, letter names, capitals and full stops, cursive writing, phonics, and story structure were all given as examples of language uses that were not previously thought necessary at infant level. Several teachers also mentioned the new need for detailed record-keeping and long-term forward planning.

5. STANDARDS OF LITERACY

5.1 Teachers' Assessments of Attainment

Reading attainment

As indicated in Section 2, pupils were classified into five categories of reading attainment by their teachers. The proportions of pupils allocated to the different categories defined are illustrated in Figure 5.1.

Figure 5.1   Classification of reading attainment by teachers

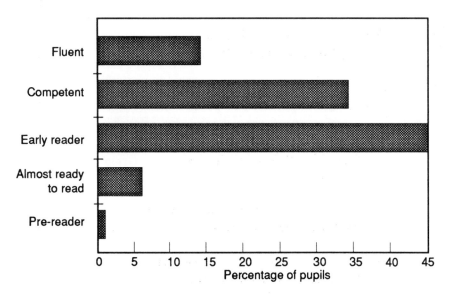

Of the sample of 742 pupils, seven per cent were said to be non-readers, that is they were either pre-readers or pupils who were almost ready to read. On the other hand, 14 per cent were classed as being fluent beyond their age in reading. In other words, twice as many pupils were categorised as falling into the highest category of reading performance as in the two lowest categories. Just under half of the pupils were said to be able to read competently or fluently, and a similar proportion were classified as emergent or early readers. Over 70 per cent of the pupils were also said to show confidence in choosing new books, which is one reflection of independence in reading.

The teachers were asked to rate their pupils in terms of levels 1 and 2 of the National Curriculum Statements of Attainment (SoAs) for reading. It was not thought appropriate to ask for information about levels of performance higher than this, as the focus of interest was the children's progression from illiteracy to the stage at which they could read fluently, which is represented by level 2. The results are given in Table 5.1. The corresponding figures are given for the approximate proportion of pupils in Year 2 who attained the different SoAs, two terms later, in a national sample of schools approached in the course of the Evaluation of the 1991 National Curriculum Assessment.

Table 5.1   Assessment of SoAs at Level 2 (Reading):
Teacher Assessment and National Evaluation

		Teacher Assessment (Term 1) %	National Evaluation (Term 3) %
Level 2	(a) Read accurately and understand straightforward signs, labels and notices.	69	85
	(b) Demonstrate knowledge of the alphabet in using word books and simple dictionaries.	80	83
	(c) Use pictures and context cues, words recognised on sight and phonic cues in reading.	84	86
	(d) Describe what has happened in a story and predict what may happen next.	78	89
	(e) Listen and respond to stories, poems and other material read aloud, expressing opinions informed by what has been read.	72	92
	(f) Read a range of material with some independence, fluency, accuracy and understanding.	47	75

To attain level 2 in the National Curriculum schema, pupils need to have attained all the SoAs listed. It is of interest that over a third of the non-readers were also classified as having attained levels 2.b, c, d and e. Over 50 per cent of the non-readers were able, for example, 'to describe what had happened in the story and to predict what may happen next' (2.d).

Three points can be made with reference to these figures. The first is that two of the criteria used to classify pupils at level 2 - knowledge of the alphabetic principle, and ability to use a range of cues in reading - are essentially skills associated with the early stages of learning to read. They are acquired by four-fifths of pupils before Year 2.

The second is that pupils evidently make rapid progress towards independent, fluent reading in Year 2. Just under half of the pupils in the survey were categorised as being able to read with independence, fluency, accuracy and understanding in the first term of the school year, whereas three-quarters of the national sample were judged to be able to do this at the end of the same year.

The third, more general, point was also made in the introduction to this report, namely that the Statements of Attainment do not designate the transitional stages of reading acquisition that pupils progress through, in moving from the stage of rudimentary literacy to the more advanced reading performance required for the attainment of level 2 of the National Curriculum. These transitional stages are discussed in section 6.

Writing attainment

Teachers in the survey schools categorised their pupils' writing attainment in terms of levels 1 and 2 of the National Curriculum Attainment Targets for writing. Their categorisations for level 2 are given in Table 5.2, together with the figures derived two terms later from the national sample of schools involved in the 1991 NFER Evaluation of Standard Assessment Tasks.

The most interesting point to note is that the proportion of pupils categorised as being able to produce writing containing grammatically punctuated sentences did not change appreciably over the period; whereas the children were judged to have improved substantially in terms of their ability to structure or compose accounts and stories. The discussion of the development of grammatical punctuation in Appendix 4 illustrates how the fluent production of coherent texts frequently precedes the mastery of the control of grammatical punctuation at sentence level, or the systematic use of upper and lower case letters. The main task of the teacher in such cases is to encourage the development of coherent and fluent writing while fostering, over the longer-term, the pupils' control over orthographic conventions, grammatical and non-grammatical punctuation, and the intricacies of the English spelling system.

The teachers also classified pupils' writing attainment in terms of a set of non-exclusive categories. These included the ability to trace and to copy writing, to practice 'scribble writing', to write with the help of support systems and to write independently (cf. Appendix 4). With reference to these categories, 35 per cent of the pupils were classified by teachers as being independent writers, and just under six out of ten were said to be able to write with some assistance, such as the use of word books. This cannot be interpreted to mean that the latter could communicate intelligibly in writing; but it indicates that they had mastered the major skills required and had reached a stage of development at which they were progressing beyond level 1 of the National Curriculum Statements of Attainment. They were able 'to use pictures, symbols or isolated letters and words or phrases to communicate meaning'. This and other evidence led the survey team to conclude that approximately one in ten pupils had not reached this stage in term 1 of Year 2. Such pupils can be said to be pre-writers. At the end of the year, in the National Evaluation programme referred to earlier, only 1 per cent of pupils in Year 2 were classified as pre-writers in this sense.

Table 5.2   Assessment of SoAs at Level 2 (Writing):
Teacher Assessment and National Evaluation

		Teacher Assessment (Term 1) %	National Evaluation (Term 3) %
Level 2 (a)	produce, independently, pieces of writing using complete sentences, some of them demarcated with capital letters or question marks.	60	57
(b)	structure sequences of real or imagined events coherently in chronological accounts.	58	88
(c)	write stories showing an understanding of the rudiments of story structure by establishing an opening, characters, and one or more events.	43	80
(d)	produce simple, coherent, non-chronological writing.	60	-

The analysis of the pupil literacy profiles indicated that there were wide variations in the pupils' knowledge about writing and their ability to write grammatical sentences. Approximately one in ten pupils were said to make systematic use of full stops, and a slightly higher proportion used capitalisation systematically. Such pupils had learnt to use the main orthographic and grammatical conventions of written English. Just over six out of ten pupils used full stops and capital letters correctly on some occasions. A similar proportion had learnt to use upper and lower case letters, with a further two out of ten using them systematically. Approximately three out of ten pupils had therefore progressed beyond the stage of being able to write isolated words, but they were not yet able to use grammatical punctuation when communicating in writing.

Writing attainment was highly correlated with reading attainment. Good readers tended to be classified as good writers (r = 0.60). Of the 36 per cent of pupils whose writing was judged to be in the top band, approximately 80 per cent were also described as being fluent or competent readers.

5.2 Stages in the Acquisition of Literacy

Children who are not yet able to read continuous prose, and who are therefore technically illiterate, may nevertheless have learnt a great deal about written language. Even among the small group of children classified by teachers as non-readers, there was a wide range of competence. Thirty per cent could sound-out unknown words; 55 per cent were able to associate letters with related sounds; and 64 per cent could sight-read familiar words. Over 60 per cent also understood common conventions of book layout; and 73 per cent had developed a concept of reading that involved interpreting the words on the page in sequence, which means they understood the concept of directionality in print. The non-readers were also developing positive attitudes to reading. Nine out of ten were said to enjoy looking at books, and six out of ten understood common conventions of book layout.

Among those classified as readers, the additional skills required for fluent, vocalised reading were being gradually acquired. Approximately three out of ten pupils, for example, tended to sub-vocalise while reading, as they used available cues to help them to read successive words. In this respect they could be regarded as having reached an 'intermediate' stage of literacy development.

The general picture, then, is that, in the judgement of their teachers, nine out of ten pupils in the first term of Year 2 had mastered the rudiments of reading. They had crossed the threshold of reading literacy. For some pupils, all this might mean in practice is that they would be able to interpret, with care, simple written statements in a familiar context, such as a poster announcing the loss of two kittens. On the other hand, approximately five out of ten pupils were judged to be able to read well, and they would be able to deal with more complex materials.

5.3 Attitudes and Attainment

A significantly higher proportion of girls than boys were classed as competent or fluent readers (55 per cent as opposed to 42 per cent); and significantly more girls than boys were categorised as able writers (43 per cent as opposed to 31 per cent). The attitudes of boys and girls to reading and writing were not markedly different at this age, although preferences for different types of reading materials had begun to develop. Seventy-nine per cent of the girls and 72 per cent of boys liked reading very much, and 59 per cent of girls and 55 per cent of boys liked writing very much. In later years, the tendency is for girls to develop more favourable attitudes to writing than boys. Ninety per cent of the girls and 74 per cent of boys enjoyed reading storybooks; whereas boys and girls had similar preferences for information books (53 per cent girls and 47 per cent boys).

One of the questions in the pupil literacy profile asked whether pupils found it hard to concentrate. Four out of ten (42 per cent) of the boys and just over two out of ten girls were said to fall into this category. Just under seven out of ten of the non-readers (67 per cent) were said to experience such difficulty in concentrating. Teachers were also asked to say whether any of the pupils were persistently disruptive. Eight per cent were said to be so, and three times as many boys as girls. None of the fluent readers was judged to be disruptive; but a quarter of the non-readers was said to be so.

Highly significant associations were found between the children's attainments in both reading and writing and their reported ability to concentrate. Non-readers and non-writers were much more likely to be said by teachers to find it difficult to concentrate than were able readers and writers. A similar strong association was found between illiteracy and the likelihood that pupils would be reported as being persistently disruptive.

5.4 Reading Standards

Finally, teachers who had been teaching Year 2 infants for three or more years were asked to say whether they had noticed any change in the reading ability of six- to seven-year-old children over the past three to five years. About a third of the total group of teachers did not respond; just under a third (33 per cent) had not noticed any change and just over a third (38 per cent) had. Among these, opinions were approximately equally divided over whether standards had declined or improved.

This question was followed by an enquiry about the possible causes or antecedents of such change. The three main factors referred to most frequently as contributing to a fall in standards were:

- a decline in the interaction between parents and children (13 per cent)

- the influence of television (12 per cent)

- a decline in reading at home (11 per cent).

There was no significant factor to which a rise in standards was attributed, the largest category relating to the fact that pupils were now exposed to a greater variety of texts (nine per cent). Most responses providing explanations for a possible improvement in reading standards referred to the value of the storybook approach to teaching reading (six per cent), to improvements in teaching, such as the use of shared or paired reading (three per cent), and to the greater involvement of parents (three per cent).

6. CONCLUSIONS

At the conclusion of this report, it seems appropriate to reflect on what has been learnt in general terms about the issues and area being studied. This concluding section points to issues and findings that the research team considered to be illuminating. They are not given in order of significance.

Writing - the 'poor cousin'

The research confirmed the wide range of performance among Year 2 children in reading and writing and more evidently the latter. The analysis of pupils' writing, which is illustrated in Appendix 4, revealed a range of achievement 'from work which would be warmly received in the nursery to some which would not be out of place in the upper years of primary school'.

One general conclusion reached, therefore, was that, while attention was legitimately being focused currently on the diagnosis and 'remedial' teaching of reading, the pressing need for similar work with reference to the teaching of writing has not been as widely recognised. Such a 'Writing Rescue' programme would apply to a larger proportion of pupils than those who have difficulties learning to read.

In commenting on the teaching of writing, it is important to note what appeared to be a concentration on 'secretarial' aspects of written work: the focus in some cases on surface features of writing as opposed to matters relating to content, form and style; the simplistic notions of 'redrafting' that prevailed in some classes; and the relative lack of exploitation of the word-processing facilities that were available to pupils in some cases, particularly with regard to redrafting.

In the main, teachers appeared to have little time to devote to the close scrutiny and discussion of children's written work. Learning to write is a very complex process. It does not help a child to have all the mistakes they make in their initial attempts to write highlighted at the same time; nor does it help to have them discounted. They need to be attended to successively. It is reasonable to suggest, for these reasons, that the sense of failure that some pupils were already experiencing with regard to their capacity as writers was, in part, a consequence of the absence of a framework for writing assessment which, if in place, would allow for attention to be focused on different aspects of written composition at appropriate stages of development.

Few teachers appeared to relate the teaching of reading and writing in a principled way. There was general acceptance of the view that the kind of writing that was done was affected by what was read; but the systematic use of what was read to provide models for writing was rare. This was perhaps one reason why pupils were typically limited in terms of the range of different types of writing that they were generally asked to undertake. The research also pointed to the lack of consensus in teachers' assumptions about their pupils' levels of performance in writing.

Differentiating between levels of performance

Meeting the individual needs of pupils for instruction in reading and writing involves, firstly, being able to differentiate between different levels of performance. Not surprisingly, many teachers find it difficult to do this; and the detailed specifications of Attainment Targets of levels 1 and 2 of the National Curriculum do not, at present, provide a clear framework for such differentiation. Briefly, the competences specified at level 1 for reading and writing relate primarily to a stage of pre-literacy; while those at level 2 relate to the accomplishment of 'fluent' reading and 'independent' writing, involving the interpretation or production of different types of written texts. The majority of children at the start of Year 2 are, however, in a transitional stage of literacy attainment, which is not directly reflected in the Statements of Attainment of the National Curriculum.

The Programmes of Study of the National Curriculum do, however, provide a valuable point of reference for teachers of reading and writing. They have been creatively applied to classroom teaching by teams of advisory teachers in the context of the Language in the National Curriculum (LINC) programme. Nevertheless, at the time this survey was undertaken, relatively few teachers in the schools visited appeared to have been involved in INSET work in the context of that programme.

In Appendix 4 an analysis of scripts written by children points to a relative lack of consensus among teachers in assigning scripts to level 1 in AT3 (writing). Yet experience in training teacher-assessors in the context of the APU surveys has shown that it is a relatively simple matter to establish a high degree of consensus among experienced teachers in assessing pupils' performance in writing and in talking (Gorman, 1986, p.39). The starting point for such consensus is the review of exemplary scripts that reflect the range of performance among the pupils concerned.

Assessment policies and procedures

In general, the assessment procedures that were used in the classes observed had little direct application to teaching strategies adopted. Six of the ten schools tested children's reading - independently of the requirements of the National Curriculum. At the same time, among teachers, we found that 'there was a general disbelief in the efficacy of formal testing'. Given the nature and purpose of many of the standardised reading tests in use, this lack of appreciation by classroom teachers of their practical value is understandable. At the same time, teachers need to acknowledge that much of the information gathered about pupils' attainments of reading and writing through informal means, is not effectively conveyed to others involved with a child's education, or, in some cases, to the child concerned. Many teachers are, moreover, aware of their own lack of expertise in identifying and teaching children with incipient reading difficulties.

Increasingly, progress in literacy acquisition is being described in terms of the Attainment Targets in the National Curriculum; but the ascription of such generalised attainments is no substitute for the detailed record of a pupil's attainments. The need for this is particularly apparent with respect to children who experience more than usual difficulty in learning to read and write.

Pupils with special educational needs

Teachers were presented with a familiar dilemma in dealing with pupils with special educational needs. This concerned the degree of 'integration' that it was possible to effect in teaching children across the ability range, while taking account of the requirements of these pupils. The extent to which additional assistance was available for children with special needs varied greatly from school to school. It was remarked in section 2 that, among the teachers involved in the case studies, there was 'an almost universal disbelief in the process of statementing'. In some authorities, such assistance for pupils with special needs, whether these were statemented or not, was evidently becoming more difficult to obtain on a systematic basis. In this respect, the findings echo those of the most recent HMI report on the teaching of reading, which drew attention to the fact that 'provision for children with reading difficulties was generally thought to be less than adequate, with many LEA support teams vulnerable to reduction or extinction' (DES, 1992).

Organisational strategies

There were marked differences between the teachers observed in terms of their competence as effective managers of children and time. Some teachers were able to keep children consistently engaged in purposeful tasks, and to exploit every available moment for its learning potential, while maintaining good rapport with the children. Such effectiveness seemed to involve a keen sense of timing: knowing when to intervene in a group, class or individual situation with new information or ideas; and when to stop and change the focus, at a point when the children were beginning to tire or lose attention. It involved, too, the skill of making use of points as they cropped up and of relating them to previous work or to the children's own circumstances; and of making cross-curricular links with maths, science, geography and other areas of the curriculum.

Effective teachers seemed to delegate responsibility within bounds, for example by allowing children to take responsibility for the appearance of their book corner. Such teachers took every reasonable opportunity to encourage children to be active rather than passive: reading their work to the class rather than having the teacher read it for them; asking peers for help or using dictionaries, rather than queuing for the teacher; and occasionally undertaking class routines normally carried out by the teacher, such as telling the class stories. This was illustrated in one school where the teacher successfully sustained a 'Show and Tell' session involving at least seven children for half an hour, during which time the attention of the class never flagged.

The most proficient teachers seemed to have established good habits in their pupils from some time in the past. Their pupils appeared to know what was expected of them, moved independently from one task to the next without explicit direction and knew what range of possibilities were open to them, when they had finished all their assigned tasks.

In summary, those teachers observed who seemed to create an atmosphere in which work was carried out effectively and with enjoyment appeared to share certain characteristics. Their manner was kind and caring. They were able to prevent noise and clamour from developing and to give the children autonomy within clear boundaries. They used spare moments well as occasions for further, informal learning, and took opportunities, through questioning, to push children towards further expression of ideas. They seemed able to combine discipline with informality. In such classrooms the atmosphere was happy, relaxed and industrious.

The classroom setting

The classrooms of effective teachers tended to have a layout that was clearly compartmentalised and 'designed' to promote opportunities for independent learning. The notices that were displayed included materials which had relevance for the pupils, such as information about their groups, or about forthcoming school events. One teacher who displayed holiday postcards sent by pupils and teachers had developed their potential by adding information about the places from which they came. In some schools, children's work was prominently displayed. Children who felt pride in their work sometimes pointed out their contributions on display. There was a marked difference in pupils' behaviour in this regard in the schools visited.

On a related issue, child-made books, both individual and group, invariably seemed to be popular with pupils. In one classroom visited, a child who was experiencing marked difficulties in writing with accuracy had nevertheless been encouraged to write and illustrate a 'book' on a film she had seen, which she read to the researcher with the confidence one might expect of an author.

Parental involvement

Schools differed greatly in the extent to which they were able or willing to draw on assistance from parents or other adults in the classroom teaching of initial literacy. In one school, for example, each child had been assigned an adult visitor, usually a parent, who gave assistance under the teacher's direction. In some schools, parents made specific contributions to the teaching programme, for example by running the school library on particular days. In two out of ten schools in the survey, however, teachers did not have the opportunity to involve parents in their work.

In a few classes, teachers had access to assistance from other teachers on a systematic basis. In such circumstances, it was theoretically possible for a form of 'partnership teaching' to develop. Partnership teaching involves pairs or groups of teachers working together inside and outside the classroom to develop a curriculum responsive to all pupils' language needs and abilities. The adoption of such teaching requires support from the senior management team in school and guidance from school policies relative to the language curriculum and the sharing of teaching resources (Bourne and McPake, 1991). The majority of teachers observed had to meet the diverse needs of pupils without trained help.

Methods of teaching reading

Most teachers claimed to use a variety of methods or approaches in teaching reading and writing. Indeed, this has been a consistent finding in all the main studies of the teaching of reading carried out in England. For example, in her 1967 NFER report, *Reading in Infant Classes*, Elizabeth Goodacre reported that 'the majority of teachers use all the main methods of teaching reading, and tend to differ principally in the order in which they introduce the basic methods and the importance they attach to any aspect at different stages of children's development'. This generalisation about practice still applies.

The 'debate' about the relative effectiveness of different methods of teaching reading was, for the most part, engendered outside the teaching profession. Among teachers in the survey sample, there was a marked consensus of opinion about the need to use different methods of teaching in the initial stages. Virtually all teachers exploited approaches that involved learning to sight-read whole words (Look and Say) in the initial stages of learning to read. Nor was any controversy evident among teachers regarding the usefulness of 'phonics' in the initial teaching of reading. All made use of methods that involved children learning to 'sound-out' letters, syllables and component parts of words.

While all teachers in the survey sample subscribed to the need for a phonics component in teaching reading, what they understood this to comprise would no doubt differ. As the recent report by the Council for the Accreditation of Teacher Education on the teaching of teachers to teach reading has emphasised, the question at issue is the relative **balance** and attention given to approaches involving an emphasis on 'phonics' or 'comprehension' (DES, 1992).

The general view of the teachers interviewed was that a minority of children in Year 2 needed systematic instruction in techniques of 'word-attack'. In most cases, the main obstacle to the provision of such instruction was not a lack of knowledge on the part of teachers, or a lack of appropriate resources (in the form of teaching materials with a systematic 'phonic' component); it was rather the lack of time available to devote to the individual instruction of non-readers and children in the early stages of learning to read while, at the same time, providing tasks that were stimulating for the majority of competent readers, and sufficiently demanding for those who were verbally gifted.

For most teachers it was time, more than any other resource, that was in short supply. This is not surprising if one considers what it was that a Year 2 teacher was likely to be doing at any moment of the day. This might involve overseeing four groups working on different tasks, making available prepared worksheets of differentiated tasks for 'high-fliers' and poor ability pupils, assisting one or two pupils on the computer, responding to the frequent demands of the SEN pupil(s), arranging to listen to individuals reading and, on occasion, dealing with a researcher observing from the corner of the room.

One difference between the situation at the present time and that which obtained when Elizabeth Goodacre conducted her survey was that, in 1967, over 80 per cent of the schools surveyed used a single reading scheme, 'Janet and John'. Whatever its limitations, the scheme provided teachers with the choice of using a 'phonic' or a 'whole-word approach' to teaching reading, a controlled vocabulary and a helpful manual of instruction. As far as the survey team is aware, there are no schemes currently available to teachers that provide such a range of support. On the other hand, no single series could provide pupils with access to what they need to learn to read, as this is a process in which 'phonological awareness, letter recognition facility, familiarity with spelling patterns, spelling-sound relations, and (knowledge of) individual words must be developed in concert with real reading and real writing and with deliberate reflection on the forms, functions, and meanings of texts' (Adams, 1990). Writing involves more complex processes still in the sense that it is more demanding to generate text than to interpret it.

In the main, the teachers interviewed had not had the opportunity to think about the characteristics of different types of texts that the children were required to read or to write as they progressed through school. Prevailing ideas about the levels of difficulty of different types of text tended to be rather simplistic, for example, books were impressionistically categorised as 'level 1' or 'level 2' books. The lack of awareness of the different language demands of areas of the curriculum was also apparent.

Group work

While the children in the classes observed were generally seated in groups, they seldom worked collaboratively within these groups; nor was it common for them to engage cooperatively in tasks which required each pupil to provide a different type of verbal input or spoken or written response. The generalisation made some years ago by the research team in the Oracle study still held true in virtually all the classes observed: 'while in most classrooms the pupils are organised in one or more seated groups – for the various activities undertaken – with few exceptions they then work largely alone, as individuals' (Galton, Simon and Croll, 1980). Sustained, individualised work is required in all areas of the curriculum but, essentially, using language is a cooperative activity. Speaking, reading and writing are best practised in cooperation and collaboration with other pupils and adults. The National Curriculum endorses a view of language that regards the development of speaking and listening, reading and writing as inextricably linked or integrated, though the presentation of Attainment Targets in separate sections relating to these applications of language to some extent obscures this insight. In the main, teachers accept in principle this functional view of language, which takes account of the ways in which the different applications of literacy and oracy are used for complementary purposes by the child, as he or she learns to communicate to different people in different situations; but the implications of that view or perspective for classroom practice and classroom organisation are neither generally appreciated nor applied.

One point needs to be made in conclusion. Whatever shortcomings there may have been in the teaching of initial literacy in the schools that participated in the study, they were all successful in one notable respect. Virtually all the children that participated in the enquiry had learnt to enjoy reading and being read to, and most had learnt to enjoy writing. This is a notable achievement.

REFERENCES

ADAMS, M. J. (1990). *Beginning to Read: Thinking and Learning about Print.* Cambridge (Mass): The MIT Press.

BOURNE, J. and MCPAKE, J. (1991). *Partnership Teaching: Cooperative Teaching Strategies for English Language Support in Multilingual Classrooms. Materials for Whole-School Inservice.* London: HMSO.

GALTON, M., SIMON, B., and CROLL, P. (1980). *Inside the Primary Classroom.* London: Routledge & Kegan Paul.

GOODACRE, E. J. (1967). *Reading in Infant Classes.* Slough: NFER

GORMAN, T. (1986). *The Framework for the Assessment of Language* (APU Survey). Windsor: NFER-NELSON.

GREAT BRITAIN. DEPARTMENT OF EDUCATION AND SCIENCE. COUNCIL FOR THE ACCREDITATION OF TEACHER EDUCATION. (1992). *Training Teachers to Teach Reading: a Review.* London: DES.

GREAT BRITAIN. DEPARTMENT OF EDUCATION AND SCIENCE. HER MAJESTY'S INSPECTORATE. (1990). *The Teaching and Learning of Reading in Primary Schools.* (HMI Report 10/91). London: DES.

GREAT BRITAIN. DEPARTMENT OF EDUCATION AND SCIENCE. HER MAJESTY'S INSPECTORATE. (1992). *The Teaching and Learning of Reading in Primary Schools 1991.* (HMI Report 42/92) London: DES.

KISPAL, A., GORMAN, T. P., and WHETTON, C. (1989). *Reading Ability Series. Teacher's Handbook.* Windsor: NFER-NELSON.

APPENDIX 1

SELECTION OF SCHOOLS AND PUPILS

The survey consisted of two national samples of schools in England and Wales. For the first sample, 164 schools were randomly selected from the register of maintained schools. To assist with the case studies, a second sample of 70 schools was selected using a multi-stage clustered design of seven LEA districts and ten schools within each selected district. For the purpose of analyses both the samples were treated as one single sample as each selected school had the same probability of selection. Up to ten pupils were randomly selected within each school for completing the Pupil Literacy Profile.

The samples were proportionately stratified by the following variables to give an appropriate and accurate representation of the school population at large:

Region:	England - North
	- Midland
	- South
	Wales (English-speaking schools only)
LEA Type:	Metropolitan
	Non-Metropolitan
School Type:	Junior
	Junior and Infants
	Others
Size of age group:	1-30 pupils
	31-60
	61-90
	91+

Response Rates

For various reasons, 15 of the original sample of 234 schools were withdrawn by the Local Education Authority from participating in the survey. Headteachers in the remainder of the sample schools were invited to take part in the study and those headteachers refusing to participate were asked for reasons for not participating.

Reasons for refusal were given by 101 headteachers - the reasons given were:

Number of schools

No time/pressure of work	75
Staff shortages/illness	7
New head/staff changes	11
School reorganisation	2
Other reasons given	6

The number of schools completing the various questionnaires were as follows:

	Number	Response rate
Total number of schools selected	234	-
Schools completing Headteacher questionnaire	122	52%
Schools completing Teacher questionnaire	115	49%
Schools completing Pupil Literacy Profiles	84	36%

The response rates for the survey were poor partly due to the time required to fill in the questionnaires and partly because the survey was targeted on those busily involved in the Key Stage 1 Standard Assessment Tasks. To reduce the effect of bias the results were weighted so as to reflect the distributions of schools and pupils in the population.

APPENDIX 2

THE PUPIL LITERACY PROFILE

The Profile fell into three parts:

Part I asked the teacher to provide information about the child under these headings:

Background information:	age, first language, nursery education etc.
Reading:	performance, behaviour, attitudes
Writing:	performance, purposes for writing, strategies, use of Information Technology
National Curriculum Attainment Targets:	which of the Statements of Attainment within levels 1 and 2 Reading and Writing had been achieved
Other background factors:	pre-school achievement, home circumstances.

These questions generally took the form of statements to be ticked if appropriate, but some were open-ended and required a fuller answer in a few lines, for example:

Please outline any factors that you feel may have affected this child's success or difficulties with reading and/or writing.

Part II involved the teacher in asking the child a series of questions and writing down his or her answers.

Questions related to the following areas.

Reading:	enjoyment of, preferences, ownership of books, self-perception as a reader, support from a parent or adult
Writing:	enjoyment of, preferences, strategies for improving performance, awareness of print in the world, support from a parent or other adult, writing done at home
Television:	enjoyment of, preferences, strategies for coping with difficulties in understanding, ownership of videotapes, time spent watching TV.

Part III replicated an exercise from Level A of the *Reading Ability Series* (Kispal, Gorman and Whetton, 1989) in order to provide an indication of reading performance and to relate results on this test to the teacher's estimate of the child's ability in terms of a five-point scale. The exercise asks children to identify information from a simple notice announcing the loss of two kittens.

APPENDIX 3

THE CASE STUDY INTERVIEWS

Interviews with teachers, in the course of the case studies in schools, covered the areas listed below.

Pupil information (period of time in school, numbers and circumstances of ESL and SEN children).

School language policy (who wrote it, how it is used).

Teaching methods (strategies and organisation).

Influences on methods:
> teaching of reading and writing;
> cross-curricular view of language;
> special needs;
> class size;
> National Curriculum.

Time given to reading.

Availability of extra help in class.

Libraries: class and school.

Other materials and resources:
> information technology;
> tape recorders;
> children's own writing.

Assessment.

APPENDIX 4

CHILDREN'S WRITING AT AGE 7

This appendix discusses examples of pupils' writing submitted by class teachers in Croydon in conjunction with the pupil literacy profile. It provides illustration of the range of performance found, with analyses of performance in relation to the writing curriculum. There is also discussion of the ways in which writing was supported and assessed in the classroom in the light of teachers' interpretations of National Curriculum Attainment Targets (ATs). Some implications for classroom practice and in-service programmes are suggested.

1. The range of performance in the subsample

A random selection of 80 completed questionnaires together with their attached samples of pupils' writing formed the basis for further analysis. Of these, 40 were from girls and 46 from boys. Within this sample, the range of performance in writing was wide, with the extremes represented by the following examples of pupils' work.

Text 1

One day an angel came to Mary and said "Mary go to Bethlehem" "you will have a baby you will call him Jesus." So the next day Joseph bought Mary a donkey to take her to Bethlehem. When they got there they Knocked on the door "is there any room" "No there is not said the inkeeper Is there any room here" they asked. "No inkeeper" "Is there any room here" said Mary for the 3rd time "yes we do have a stable that you could try" "Thank you" said Joseph. "My wife is going to have a baby to night."

Just before Mary fell asleep she had a baby The next day a shepherd Saw an angel. He told the others what the angel had Said. Then said "we must take a present for the baby King!" "Lets take a lamb as a present." "When they got Lets they gave him a there. Three kings were follwing a star. They brought some gifts of gold, frankincense and myrrh. They gave it to the baby king.

Wayne

Text 2

I bew DKRw dewyb oeue
be Mmoeu ke Ie nwe gew Jews
For a present

Lisa

As can be seen from these two scripts, children aged seven vary as writers between those who are well able to communicate their meaning in writing, producing extended texts which are quite comprehensible and interesting to an outside reader, and those whose attempts at writing are insufficiently systematic for anyone other than a sympathetic reader, present at the time of writing, to make sense of what a child has written after the event.

Lisa's teacher described her current writing performance as 'scribble writing' but becoming 'able to generate real symbols or letters', whereas Wayne's teacher commented 'working at level 3'. The children themselves showed contrasting attitudes to writing, with Wayne indicating the most positive attitudes, and Lisa the most negative. Both children declared that they did not find it difficult to write; Wayne gave no further explanation of this, but Lisa's reply, 'because I leave gaps between my words', is suggestive of the focus of her attention at this earlier stage of development, as is her criterion for her 'best piece of writing' (entitled 'things about me') : 'it looked good'. Wayne judged his best piece to have been 'a story about a tree' because it was 'the first proper story I ever wrote'. For Lisa, the question, 'what is writing?', produced the answer 'letters', for Wayne, the answer 'words'. Both children had someone at home to write with them, in Lisa's case a sister, in Wayne's, his father, but whereas Wayne was recorded as writing all the types of texts suggested on the pupil literacy profile, Lisa's writing was limited to her own name and 'stories'. For the teacher in charge of a mixed ability class, the pedagogic problems posed by these extremes are considerable, demanding different forms of support, different emphases within common programmes of study, and a flexible strategy of class organisation.

2. Interpreting achievement in terms of the National Curriculum SoAs

In order to place the subsample of scripts in the more general context of writing performance across the LEA, we can refer to the ways in which teachers seemed to be interpreting the National Curriculum SoAs for levels 1 and 2, as presented on the questionnaire. Bearing in mind that these individual statements are not mutually exclusive, and that assessments of individual children are likely to be made with reference to more than one statement, the following patterns emerged:

Level	Statements of Attainment	% pupils said to have attained SoA
Level 1(a)	able to use pictures, symbols or isolated letters, words or phrases to communicate meaning.	78
Level 2(a)	produce, independently, pieces of writing using complete sentences, some of them demarcated with capital letters or question marks.	50
(b)	structure sequences of real or imagined events coherently in chronological accounts.	66
(c)	write stories showing an understanding of the rudiments of story structure by establishing an opening, characters, and one or more events.	46
(d)	produce simple, coherent, non-chronological writing.	59

Several considerations need to be borne in mind when interpreting these figures, with respect to both high and low performance. Firstly, teachers were not asked to assess their children with respect to level 3. Therefore, 'invisible' within the sample as a whole there are likely to be some children (nationally about 10 to 15 per cent) who are performing at level 3 in at least some respects. Secondly, it is apparent from the pupil literacy profiles and their attached samples of work that where children have developed beyond the stage of rudimentary communication in writing, teachers tend to ignore level 1. Thus, the fact that 78 per cent of children are stated to be at level 1 does not mean that approximately 20 per cent of children were not yet at level 1, any more than it means that a group of this size was uniquely at level 1, that is 'able to use pictures, symbols or isolated letters, words or phrases to communicate meaning'. From the evidence of the subsample, it appeared that there were approximately 13 per cent of pupils assessed by their teachers as level 1 (the nature of the writing samples for these

52

children is discussed below). We need also to remember that the study took place several months before the administration of formal Standard Assessment Tasks, and therefore assessments made in mid-autumn should logically be a little lower than the eventual results.

The figures above provide an interesting indication of where teachers perceived some of children's difficulties with writing to lie. Taking the responses for level 2 SoAs, we can see that half of the age group were thought to be able to 'produce, independently, pieces of writing using complete sentences, some of them demarcated with capital letters or question marks'. Less than half of the children were described as able to 'write stories showing an understanding of the rudiments of story structure by establishing an opening, characters, and one or more events'. By contrast, two thirds of the age group were thought to be able to 'structure sequences of real or imagined events coherently in chronological accounts', and slightly fewer were stated to be able to 'produce simple, coherent, non-chronological writing'. Further discussion of other aspects of the writing curriculum, as revealed by the subsample, is undertaken below.

3. Teachers' assessments and aspects of performance

3.1 *Supported writing*

Teachers were asked on the pupil literacy profile to make their own assessment of each child's current level of writing performance in terms of:

- dictating texts which s/he then traces

- dictating texts which s/he then copies underneath

- 'scribble writing'

- ability to generate real symbols or letters

- writing with the help of support systems, e.g. word books

- writing independently.

A further question sought information about the child's occasional or systematic use of full stops, upper and lower case, and capitalisation to start a sentence. At this age, practically no children were considered by their teachers to be 'writing [totally] independently', that is without the help of some forms of support systems, and less than half were judged to be systematically using key features of grammatical punctuation – responses which are in line with the broad trend of the teachers' assessments made in relation to National Curriculum Attainment Targets.

Not explicitly mentioned as a means of support for **writing** is of course **reading**, and the importance of this factor is picked up in the significant patterns of correlation between reading and writing reported earlier.

Answers to the one question indicated that teachers were mainly assessing pupils' current writing performance by considering both the ability 'to generate real symbols or letters' and 'writing with the help of support systems, e.g. word books', or the latter statement in combination with 'writing independently'. In the subsample analysed, this kind of overlapping combination was shown by the fact that 63 pupils were noted as writing with some support, of whom approximately half were either also classified as generators of symbols or letters, or also 'writing independently'. A further scrutiny of these figures showed that 24 boys were classified as generators of symbols or letters, while only ten girls were said to be still at this stage of development. 'Scribble writing' was checked in a few cases, but the practice of tracing or copying dictated texts was not mentioned as part of any child's development. (This did not altogether accord with children's own reports about their writing experiences.) Evidence of deliberately structured writing practice – completing gapped sentences and the provision of vocabulary items – was seen in texts like the one below. There was widespread evidence of teacher-supplied 'words', but few pupils appeared to be explicitly practising writing to model sentences.

Monday 26th November — Text 3
It is a rainy day. We have walked to school and we all wet.
On Saturday I went to muy noo haus. I did sum wook.

3.2 Development of grammatical punctuation

Answers to the question concerning the frequency of use of features of grammatical punctuation revealed that systematic use of full stops, upper and lower case, and capitalisation to start a sentence was found in the work of about one in ten pupils. (There was a tendency for girls' work to be more often exemplary than boys'.) Occasional use of these features was noted as likely in the work of about five in ten pupils. For a sizeable proportion of the sample, no response was given to any of these questions, implying that about three in ten pupils were producing writing which contained less than occasional evidence of such features, as indeed appears to be corroborated by the interpretation of National Curriculum Attainment Targets, level 2 (a).

As an example of the non-coincidence of fluent writing and control of grammatical punctuation, the following letter stands for many other instances in the sample, which read coherently yet are devoid of both full stops and the systematic use of upper and lower case:

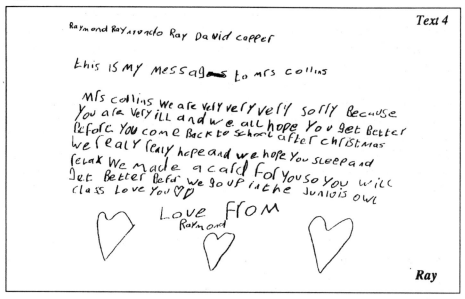

Text 4

Raymond Ray and do Ray David copper

this is my message to mrs collins

Mrs collins We are very very very sorry Because You are Very ill and we all hope You get Better Before You come Back to school after christmas We realy realy hope and we hope You sleep and relax We made a card for You so you will Jet Better befor we go up in the Juniors owl class Love You

Love FROM
Raymond

Ray

Such features do start to appear in the work of young children, often displaying a non-standard logic, as is shown by Bill's account of his visit to Norfolk:

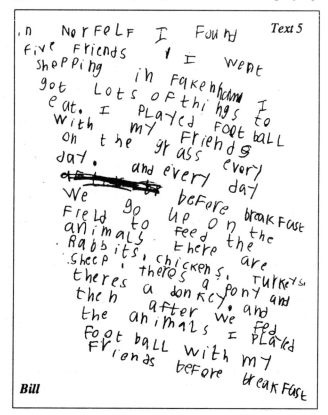

Text 5

in NorFelF I Found five Friends I I went shopping in Fakenham I got Lots of things to eat. I Played Foot ball With my Friends on the grass every day. and every day

We go up on the Field to Feed the animals there are Rabbits, chickens, Turkeys, Sheep, theres a pony and then a donkey. and the after we Fed the animals I Played Foot ball with my Friends before break Fast

Bill

55

Again, the handwriting style mixes upper and lower case letters without regard to position in word or to the place of words in the whole text, but two forms of punctuation (full stop and comma) are used to help articulate the development of meaning. Thus, the first full stop comes after the general scene-setting, and successive ones divide the activities of playing football, feeding the animals, and playing football again, with commas appearing quite appropriately in the separation of kinds of animals in the list.

The tendency of young writers to use the full stop first to demarcate sections of the text (treating them more like 'utterances' or 'turns' in speech) is a promising sign of active attention to the role of punctuation in writing, and usually runs counter to more traditional ways of encouraging sentence punctuation. Working more from knowledge of spoken language than written, 'spontaneous' punctuation frequently operates at the level of paragraph rather than sentence division, and is therefore suggestive of new ways of approaching this aspect of text structure in the early years.

To represent the 50 per cent of children in the whole sample who were able to 'write in clear sentences that are punctuated with capital letters and full stop', Julie's work is reproduced below:

> On Saturday I went to Kate's fireworks party. We had some cakes I had one pees Then it was time for the fireworks First we had a rockit and some little things and they were Spining. We had 5 rockets The nxest one was a romen candal. It Sprade in all dissrant colers the colors were blue yellow and gold Then we had a little romen candal. It had blue and gold. We had another rocket. This time it was a red one. It Shawed with red and gold. Then we had another rocket It was a bytical one It had green and gold we had croeoge firework Then we had the last firework this time it was red blue and gold it made a big bang Then we went in to have tea. I had a potato Some beans and Some little bits of cheese. For pooding I had Some ice Cream and apple cruble. I had a cup of lemon.
>
> *Text 6*

While not wishing to detract from the high achievement demonstrated by this pupil, it may be suggested that as with all processes of learning, there may be a point when a feature is overlearnt. Perhaps the next stage for Julie might be not to unlearn the full stop but to learn a greater variety of punctuation devices in order to be able to control shades of meaning and degrees of emphasis in her writing. The problem with using a series of short declarative sentences is that all statements are read with the same amount of certainty, each one potentially a free-standing truth. An awareness of the intonation contours of speech would also be helpful in Julie's case as a reference point in identifying more of the resources of English punctuation.

4.   Problems with making sense of level 1: writing as a system or communicating meaning

The range of achievements potentially qualifying for the National Curriculum AT 3, level 1 are difficult to interpret, because of the great difference in practice between trying to make sense of a text in which the child has used 'pictures, symbols or isolated letters' as compared with one in which recognisable words and phrases appear. Faced only with the former, one might well attribute meaning-making behaviour to the child, but not be at all sure of how such intentions are carried by the text. Analysis of the subsample of scripts highlights certain problems in the assignment of level 1, especially when this is read without simultaneous reference to writing ATs 4 and 5 (spelling and handwriting).

AT 4 provides three strands for consideration at level 1, i.e.
   a) begin to show an understanding of the difference between drawing and writing, and between numbers and letters;
   b) write some letter shapes in response to speech sounds and letter names;
   c) use at least single letters or groups of letters to represent whole words or parts of words.

AT 5 indicates that pupils should
   a) begin to form letters with some control over the size, shape and orientation of letters or lines of writing.

Writing analysed in the subsample indicated that all children had achieved AT4 level 1, and, given some latitude in the interpretation of 'some control', had likewise achieved level 1, AT5. Texts such as Text 7 (below) might prove interesting for teachers to discuss with reference to AT5.

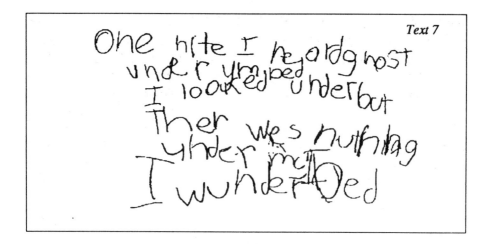

Text 7

One nite I herd g host
under my bed
I looked under but
Ther wes nuthing
under my bed
I wunderd ed

5. Examples of writing assessed by teachers as representing AT3 Level 1

The assignment of level 1, AT 3 seemed more controversial between teachers. Thus we find level 1 exemplified by scripts as diverse as the following:

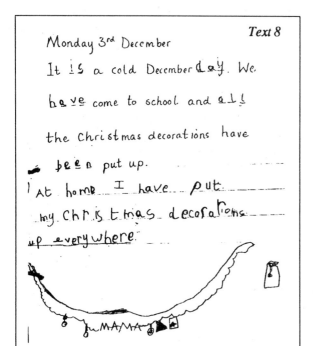

Text 8

Monday 3rd December

It is a cold December day. We

have come to school and all

the Christmas decorations have

been put up.

At home I have put

my Christmas decorations

up everywhere.

Text 9

Bes ar wos wen my
ddd Gee weh ow my ne
an was I hat w
w

Text 10

It is a nice hot day and me and my friend
and we played with the doll and played with
with the grils and stia yel

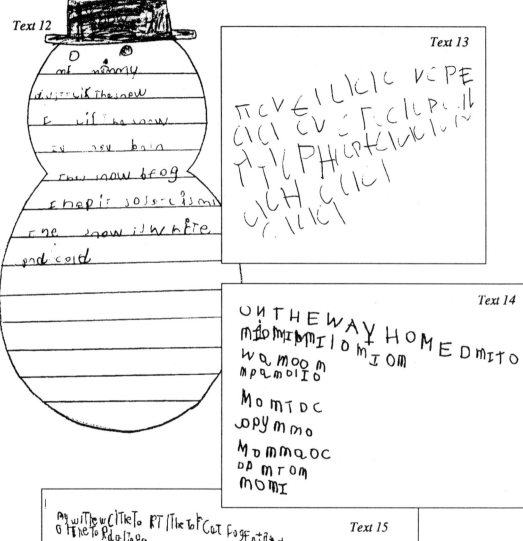

Text 11

I WET to MI GRANES hos

Text 12

mf nimmy
divjttik The snow
k uil be snow
iv nsw bain
rou snow bfog
r hepir sossrcäsmi
r ye snow is white
and cold

Text 13

π c v E I LICIC VCPE
CICI CV CT CICILPIL
π ICPHICPTCIVCIVN
CICH CICI
CIICI

Text 14

ON THE WAY HOME D MITO
MIO MIMMI I O M J OM
WA MOO M
MPAMOIIO

MO MTDC
OPY mmo
MO MMAOC
PP MTOM
MOMI

Text 15

My wiTheW CITheTo RT ITheToF CaT FoGFotdet.
o ITheTo Rda IIoRMGRS NmISLTheILToNib.

AS ChAISTRDA   KWADSI ASRA
A MA BARRY D   RAKSTIAWDR   PARRYBADMDAYShkh
                                 NwiEwESRIIhoND

59

Perhaps the most salient feature of the achievements which AT3 aims to describe is that of the ability to use writing in a systematic way to communicate meaning, from the very beginnings through to the more advanced stages of literacy. By contrast, it is possible to fulfil the requirements of level 1 for AT 4 and 5 without communicating meaning, in the sense of producing text which is comprehensible to an outside reader, and hence independent of its writer and context. For the teacher intimately connected with the context and the child, some form of meaning can usually be inferred – only in the case of Text 9 did the teacher comment that the work could not be read back. Yet from the point of view of working with the SoAs in a diagnostic fashion, it would seem to make good sense to reserve the ascription of AT3 level 1 for texts in which communicative intentions are transparent to more than one sympathetic reader, while still crediting the child with achievements on ATs 4 and 5 where these are evident.

6.   Attitudes to writing held by children at the initial stages of literacy

Only three of the 13 children whose writing was assessed at level 1 registered themselves as feeling unhappy about writing. The lack of a direct connection between motivation to write and performance level is perhaps symptomatic of the initial stages of literacy, when children are entitled and indeed encouraged to believe that they will eventually succeed. It is undoubtedly important to foster children's commitment and enthusiasm through these often difficult early stages, given the overwhelming evidence from studies of older populations of readers and writers concerning the link between negative attitudes and low performance.

Nine of the 'level 1' children said that they found writing difficult. Reasons for the difficulty related mostly to problems with spelling and handwriting:

> *all the time you have to sound out letters and make sure you do finger spaces;*
>
> *it's hard to write small writing;*
>
> *the words are long;*
>
> *I get stuck on words I can't spell;*
>
> *I don't know all the words;*
>
> *some words are hard;*
>
> *the letters are hard;*
>
> *the noise in the room (when it's not writing workshop);*
>
> *I don't feel very well when I write. I get worried about it.*

Those who alleged no difficulty seemed to have some kind of security system to hand:

> *because you can see it in your book (copywriting)*
>
> *it's easy to write the letters (favourite writing: copying books)*
>
> *because the teacher teached me*
>
> *because I leave spaces between my words.*

The children's own judgements of what counted as their best writing had to do with the length of words or of the whole text – 'because the words are long'/ 'when I write right down to the bottom of the page' – and with correctness: 'having the words in a book [to copy from]', 'it was neat', 'it was little writing', 'nice small letters', 'I sounded out all the letters and got them all right', 'writing was good'. Their comments on what helped them learn to write stressed handwriting practice and learning to spell: 'if you do the sounds', playing 'I spy', and copying words. One child suggested watching mum and dad, another recommended 'eat proper food'. However, references to thinking and to reading – 'think in our head'; 'think hard, look at books, or ask a friend to help'; 'think and look at the letters on the wall'; 'I look in books for words I read' – indicated an intuitive grasp of the fact that learning to write, unlike learning to speak, involves sustained concentration in which interaction with reader(s) becomes internalised and silent.

Comments from these children about what they need to learn in order to write are very much focused on the strands of Writing ATs 4 and 5, more than on those aspects of AT3 which conceptualise writing as a communicative system involving different readers and different purposes. From work with older populations of children, it has been found that such a focus of attention is the norm rather than the exception. For children still at the early stages of literacy development, our concern should be to monitor the extent to which their perceptions about writing expand with their competence as communicators. There were suggestions from the subsample that this domain of understanding was not keeping pace with outcomes in writing, since narrowly focused attitudes were pervasive, irrespective of levels of performance in writing. Nevertheless, all children were aware of environmental print, most were said to write a variety of things at home, and all had some family member willing to write with them, so there are positive foundations to build on.

7.   Discrepancies in the interpretation of other ATs

While it is preferable to have more than one piece of work on which to judge a child's level of performance in writing, there were some cases in which teachers' assessments of levels did not seem intuitively supported by the samples provided. The following three pieces of work were written by children whose teachers ticked **all** the SoAs (levels 1 and 2) on their behalf.

Text 16

A pizza for the Turtles

I wod put sum tmutsos and cheese and clkis and sum fedapkand sum chofolahle.

Text 17

I like playing with my Sister and friend Nicole.
We have fun at playing . My Mummy is very nice
Mummy is very nice to us We like playing with
Mummy

Text 18

Christmas is a goop time is goop for Jesus and Mere and Joesef Youseef Children O. Poh men presenes Sarta. is cio

This would seem an over-optimistic reading, relative to other work in the subsample. For example, Text 19 was from a pupil whose teacher more soberly assessed her writing as 'working towards 2c and developing . . . story writing'.

Bearing in mind teachers have only recently had opportunities to work towards a consensus view of achievements in writing at these early stages, it is to be expected that their judgements will to some extent differ across an LEA. The indications from the subsample of writing studied are that details of the range of performance are at risk of being blurred by the lack of comparative data. It is quite clear from the sample texts that early-years teachers in the LEA place different emphases on features of the writing system, although the same variation does not show so clearly in the types of text written. Moderation procedures, which entail teachers from different schools meeting to discuss and compare the writing produced in their individual classrooms, would do much to clarify matters in this respect. Procedures of this kind would in turn help to refine the formulation of the ATs themselves, which were after all proposed more as hypotheses than as the result of empirical studies of writing development over 11 years of compulsory schooling.

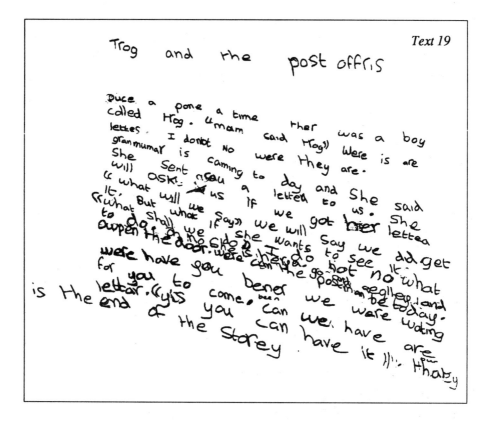

Text 19

8. The nature of the writing curriculum as represented by the subsample

Since the introduction of the National Curriculum for English, there has been renewed emphasis placed on the need for children to undertake a broad range of writing from the earliest stages of schooling. The programmes of study for KS1 contain numerous suggestions as to the types of and contexts for writing which may appropriately be tackled by this age group. It is of interest, therefore, to report on teachers' replies to the question on the pupil literacy profile, which specifically asked about the forms of writing undertaken by each child in the day-to-day work of the classroom.

8.1 *Predominance of 'recounts'*

The questionnaire suggested nine possible forms of writing and teachers checked most of these options for most pupils: stories (93 per cent), descriptions (88 per cent), reports (75 per cent), books (69 per cent), lists (76 per cent), letters (86 per cent), charts and graphs (68 per cent), cards (88 per cent), poetry (49 per cent). However, the subsample did not contain a range of types of writing in the proportions in which they were said to be undertaken (one example of a poem was provided). Overall, the collection of work was dominated by the type of writing characterised in the SoAs as '[coherent] sequences of real or imagined events in chronological accounts'. Thus, the many instances of writing anecdotal accounts of personal experience as well as the writing that was done to retell a Christmas story, or the events of other stories that had figured in the experience of the class, all fell into this category.

Such texts have aptly been described as 'recounts' to distinguish them from fully fledged 'stories', which show a more complex narrative structure in which the sequence of events is deliberately elaborated and characters are introduced and developed (the achievements in writing suggested by AT3, level 2 (c) and level 3 (c)). Despite an increasing amount of attention in in-service courses to ways of developing a more precise and helpful metalanguage for the description of written texts, the label 'story' is still applied to all kinds of writing - hence the claim that almost all children in the sample wrote stories.

Judging by the nature of scripts in the subsample, it would appear that children's experience of writing 'simple, non-chronological texts' was also rather narrow. With some exceptions, this category seemed mainly to comprise letters of request (to Santa) or forms of journal writing which served briefly to record and comment on doings and happenings out of school.

8.2 *Coincidence of subject matter for writing*

Given that the sample was collected in the months of November/December of the autumn term, there was a perhaps predictable coincidence of subject matter for a lot of the writing: Bonfire Night, letters to Santa, the Nativity story, snowmen. When left to choose topics unaided, the writing of boys and girls showed familiar stereotypical differences. Thus, the topic of favourite toys or pastimes, seemed to prompt girls to write about dolls and friends, boys to write about transformers and other machines. Descriptive writing based on snow was almost entirely concocted, considering the untraditional mildness of the early winter weather in 1991. There seemed to be an underexploitation of the possibilities for descriptive writing likely to have formed part of first-hand experience in the course of several weeks' schooling.

Much more than types of writing are being implicitly learnt here: the range of subject matter 'chosen' serves to reinforce certain prevailing cultural assumptions about writing and about childhood with scant reference to other traditions. Within the confines of a single classroom, the range of subject matter for writing may appear solely a matter of individual choice, but when the work of many schools is seen to conform to the same patterns, we can surely question the extent to which such practices may be desirable or deliberate.

By comparison with the plethora of news-like comments about personal experience and the rehearsal of mainstream stories and legends, there was sparse representation of writing from 'scientific' parts of the curriculum, which might perhaps have been done in relation to close observation, experimental work, or for the purpose of making sense of new learning. In this category we found some explanatory texts – one explaining the procedure of making a megaphone, another explaining how the ear acts as an advance warning signal of danger – plus a group of scripts arising from work on the topic of 'my body' and variously concerned to comment on the functions of bodily parts and their upkeep. Examples of this group of scripts are reproduced below.

The significance of expository writing is not so much that it deals with 'Science' but that, because of the pattern of language choices engaged by such writing, it has an important place in a child's written repertoire across the curriculum. In order to tell how something works or is made, or to report on the nature of a process or a class of phenonemon, the resources of language needed differ from those typically used to construct stories or personal anecdotes. Instead of a focus on persons (I, we, or named characters) and their actions, thoughts and feelings, expository writing switches attention to things or processes (megaphone, ear, brain, swimming). Expository texts move towards impersonal, generalised accounts of the world, something evident in the choice of present ('timeless') tense rather than past tense, with its connotation of a single, specific occurrence.

Text 20

We can Find out Where danger is looking From with our sens of hehing it is very hard to get the meesidge if the sonde is to qviet and the Brain con't make out if it is danyen or not so the ear Haste work evany Hardof.

Kate

HOW to make a megaphene

I got a piece of Paper and i stareed to RalL It. It starts to RalL a little bet and then it gets bigger and bigger and then you gule It and then you have got and to push it down and then you have a megaPhone

I went swimming
Swimming Helps us to get fit

The work of the three pupils above illustrates degrees of accomplishment in these respects. Paul, writing about the megaphone, begins with a specific, personal statement, then generalises his experience by changing tenses and adopting the inclusive pronoun 'you'. Amy, explaining the benefits of swimming, follows her personal remark not by an attitudinal comment (e.g. 'I like swimming very much') as would be typical in most journal or 'news' writing, but by a general authoritative statement on swimming itself. Kate, the most adept of these three writers, writes a coherent explanation of the ear's function, beginning with the general statement 'we can', and sustaining the level of generality through a series of inclusive reference: 'our sense of hearing', 'the sender', 'the message', 'the brain', 'the ear'. Also notable is her secure handling of the 'if ..., so...' structure needed to establish cause and effect relations. Here too is a point of contrast with chronologically ordered texts: an explanation or exposition is not dependent upon time for its ordering, but on the writer's judgement about logical and appropriate sequencing of contrast. The need to order parts of a text by virtue of their logical relations demands the use of conjunctions other than 'and' or 'then' (a development not yet mastered by Paul).

9.   Concluding comments

The subsample of writing collected from seven-year-old pupils has revealed much about the nature of writing performance at this stage of schooling. Most striking is the range of achievement shown, from work which would be warmly received in the nursery to some which would not be out of place in the upper years of primary school.

Aside from the questions about **why** such differences are found (and a study like this can scarcely do more than sketch out areas for potential investigation), there is the more pressing question of **how** to address such differences in the daily work of the classroom.

Related to both questions would seem to be a major priority for in-service work: providing occasions for teachers to meet and discuss their children's work in order to establish a broader perspective on current outcomes and future strategies. From the evidence of the subsample of scripts, it is apparent that teachers across the LEA are operating quite a diversity of approaches to the teaching of writing – a perception that comes less from self reports than from the evidence of children's work. At the same time, a consensus view of a curriculum for writing seems to be working at least implicitly across a diversity of teaching styles. For example, the pattern emerging from teachers' assessment of writing in relation to National Curriculum Attainment Targets suggests that children aged seven are most proficient at writing (simple) chronological and non-chronological texts. As pointed out earlier, these two types predominated in the subsample, to the exclusion of attempts to develop other forms of (chronological) narrative, or more purposeful expository writing. We might therefore ask whether children are being given a sufficiently wide range of models of writing to enable them to develop beyond this stage, or whether there is an artificial ceiling on achievement in this respect.

Guided discussion about these issues would serve to enhance thinking about the content, range and purpose of children's writing, and from such sharing of expertise, perhaps more could be anticipated by way of positive outcomes in the classroom.

Further reading

GORMAN, T.P. (1987). *Pupils' Attitudes to Reading*. Windsor: NFER-NELSON.

GORMAN, T. P., WHITE, J., BROOKS, G. and KISPAL, A. (1988). *Language Performance in Schools. Review of APU Language Monitoring 1979-83*.

GORMAN, T.P., WHITE, J., BROOKS, G., KISPAL, A. and TATE, A. (1991). *Assessment Matters No.4. Language for Learning: a Report of the 1988 APU Language Surveys*. London: SEAC.

WHITE, J. (1987). *Pupils' Attitudes to Writing*. Windsor: NFER-NELSON.

WHITE, J. (1991). 'What does Simon know about writing?' In: *English in Education*, NATE, Spring 1991.